Black Hawk and the War of 1832

REMOVAL IN THE NORTH

LANDMARK EVENTS IN
NATIVE AMERICAN HISTORY

Black Hawk and the War of 1832

REMOVAL IN THE NORTH

JOHN P. BOWES
Assistant Professor of History
Eastern Kentucky University

SERIES EDITOR: PAUL C. ROSIER
Assistant Professor of History
Villanova University

CHELSEA HOUSE
PUBLISHERS
An imprint of Infobase Publishing

Cover: The 1832 Battle of Bad Axe, in which approximately 300 members of Black Hawk's band were killed, is depicted in this woodcut.

BLACK HAWK AND THE WAR OF 1832: Removal in the North

Copyright © 2007 by Infobase Publishing

Chelsea House
An imprint of Infobase Publishing
132 West 31st Street
New York NY 10001

Library of Congress Cataloging-in-Publication Data
Bowes, John P., 1973-
  Black Hawk and the War of 1832 : removal in the north / John P. Bowes.
    p. cm. — (Landmark events in Native American history)
  Includes bibliographical references and index.
  ISBN-13: 978-0-7910-9342-9 (hardcover)
  ISBN-10: 0-7910-9342-5 (hardcover)
  1. Black Hawk, Sauk chief, 1767-1838. 2. Sauk Indians—Kings and rulers—Biography. 3. Black Hawk War, 1832. I. Title. II. Series.
  E83.83.B636 2007
  973.5'6—dc22   2007004927

You can find Chelsea House on the World Wide Web at
http://www.chelseahouse.com

Series design by Erika K. Arroyo
Cover design by Ben Peterson

Printed in the United States of America

Bang NMSG 10 9 8 7 6 5 4 3 2 1

This book is printed on acid-free paper.

All links and Web addresses were checked and verified to be correct at the time of publication. Because of the dynamic nature of the Web, some addresses and links may have changed since publication and may no longer be valid.

Contents

American Expansion and Removal

PRESIDENT ANDREW JACKSON DELIVERED HIS FIRST annual address nearly five decades after the end of the American Revolution. In his speech, he explained how federal Indian policy often contradicted itself during those early years of the nation. "It has long been the policy of Government to introduce among them the arts of civilization," he asserted, "in the hope of gradually reclaiming them from a wandering life. This policy has, however, been coupled with another wholly incompatible with its success. Professing a desire to civilize and settle them, we have at the same time lost no opportunity to purchase their lands and thrust them farther into the wilderness." Jackson's speech summarized well the problems of federal policy up to that point in time. But the president also used the opportunity to set the stage for a new policy focused on removal. This policy would address one of the key issues that had not been acted upon by the country's leaders—the relationship between the new nation and its original inhabitants.

In the late 1780s, James Madison, Alexander Hamilton, and others had successfully drafted and promoted the Constitution, which became the framework for the new republic. The country's leaders quickly addressed some of the more critical issues, but they left others to future leaders to debate and resolve. Months of debate led to a government built on the powers of the executive, legislative, and judicial branches. At the same time, these leaders avoided making any definitive statements on other issues, notably slavery.

In addition, both federal officials and U.S. citizens were undecided over the proper place of Indian tribes and individuals within the new nation. From the American Revolution onward, the United States struggled to define and state its core principles.

What would be the policy of the young country toward the Indians living east and west of the Appalachian Mountains? Many eastern Indians had allied with the British during the American Revolution. These Indians had hoped that their efforts could halt the advance of Anglo-American settlers. However, the American victory meant that the Cherokee, Shawnee, Iroquois, Delaware, and other tribes would have to negotiate with the new nation on the continent. And U.S. officials had to decide where those same Indians would fit into this new nation.

Numerous voices contributed to this debate. In 1783, the Treaty of Paris brought an end to the American Revolution. In 1830, Congress passed the Indian Removal Act. During the five decades in between, presidents, cabinet members, congressmen, and Indian leaders all had their say. They talked about who owned the land and who had the right to sell the land. Most important, they debated whether Americans and Indians could peacefully coexist. Not only did Indians and Americans rarely see eye to eye, but there was also disagreement within Anglo-America itself.

And yet, federal officials and U.S. citizens did support a few basic points. First, all non-Indian residents of the eastern states and the growing western territories agreed that some solution was necessary to establish peaceful relations between the two peoples. Second, they recognized that land use and land ownership were the central causes of conflict. Third and finally, all non-Indians believed that the U.S. government and the American people knew what was best for the Indians.

Despite these points of agreement, early Indian policy was not always consistent. From the 1780s to the 1820s, the U.S. government instituted several different plans, but land policies, government trading houses, and missionary work did not resolve the most pressing issue. Cherokee, Creek, Shawnee, Potawatomi, and other Indian communities still lived on lands coveted by American settlers. By the late 1820s, many Americans believed that the removal of eastern Indian tribes presented the best and only solution to this problem.

FEDERAL INDIAN POLICY

Federal policy in the decades after the American Revolution reflected the larger debates among U.S. officials and citizens regarding American Indians. From the administration of George Washington to that of James Monroe, the discussions revolved around the western territories, the fur trade, and the prevailing views about civilization.

At the end of the American Revolution, the new government was in debt and did not have a powerful army. Thousands of its citizens also wanted to settle the lands west of the Appalachian Mountains. The British government had once attempted to restrict the expansion of the colonies. But the defeat of the British meant that such restrictions had been removed. All of these circumstances influenced the U.S. government's approach to Indian affairs from the 1780s forward.

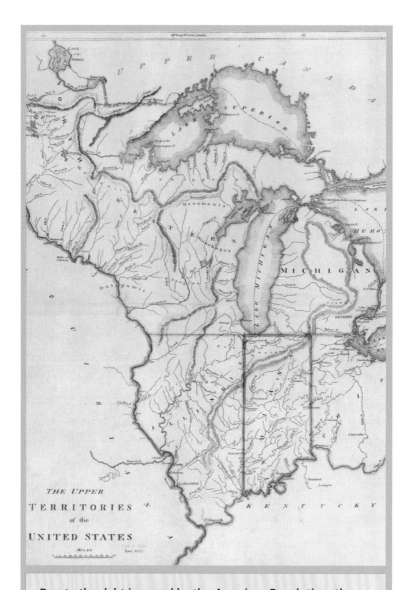

Due to the debt incurred by the American Revolution, the
U.S. government needed a way to generate revenue; as
a result, Congress adopted the Land Ordinance of 1785.
Under the plan, the U.S. government sold land to those
citizens who wished to move to what became known as
the Northwest Territory—the present-day states of Ohio,
Indiana, Michigan, Illinois, and Wisconsin.

To pay its debts and satisfy its citizens, the federal government first chose to survey and sell western lands. Two specific pieces of legislation established the particulars of the policies. The Land Ordinance of 1785 established a procedure for the survey of townships that were each 36 square miles. The townships were further divided into one-square mile sections. These sections of land would be given to American veterans of the Revolution, and the remaining sections were sold at public auction and the government received the profits. The Northwest Ordinance of 1787 built upon the 1785 legislation, providing for the organization of three to five states out of the Northwest Territory. The territory targeted by this ordinance eventually became the states of Ohio, Indiana, Michigan, Illinois, and Wisconsin.

When Congress passed these two land ordinances, one significant problem remained. In the 1780s, the lands encompassed by the Northwest Territory were still claimed by Shawnee, Delaware, Potawatomi, Wyandot, and other Indian tribes. Secretary of War Henry Knox argued that the United States did not have the strength to fight those Indians; nor could the U.S. government prevent white settlers from moving into the Northwest Territory. Knox recommended that federal officials sign treaties with the Indians for their land. But the treaties signed in the 1780s did not persuade Ohio Indians to surrender their claims to the land. Instead they resisted the arrival of Anglo-American settlers over the following decade.

In the 1790s, the U.S. government initiated a second set of policies intended to improve relations between the two groups. Congress approved the Trade and Intercourse Act in 1790 and passed several revised versions of that legislation throughout the following several decades. These laws targeted the interaction between U.S. citizens and American Indians. They regulated trade relations, criminal actions, and trespassing on Indian lands. These laws also made the federal government the ultimate authority in Indian affairs.

Related policies illustrated two other important trends. First, U.S. officials wanted to undermine the influence of British and Spanish traders by establishing a series of trading posts funded and operated by the government. These posts were established so that Indians would become better friends with the U.S. government, which could better control Indian access to goods. A series of more than 20 trading posts operated between 1795 and 1822, but the quality of the goods at these posts could never match that of the British merchants. Thus this system was never a financial success.

The second related policy focused on converting Indians to Western ideas about civilization. In 1791, President George Washington promoted a "system corresponding with the mild principles of religion and philanthropy toward" the Indians.[1] During the following three decades, both federal officials and Christian missionaries acted on this vision. Missionaries from several different Christian denominations lived and worked with Indian tribes throughout the eastern United States and tried to persuade those communities to change their way of life. These men and women wanted Indians to convert to Christianity and rely more on agriculture for their subsistence. In 1819, Congress passed the Civilization Fund Act, which provided money to support these efforts.

REGIONAL ENCOUNTERS AND SUPPORT FOR REMOVAL

By the 1820s, the Anglo-American public began to support the concept of removal. It had been a gradual process. The Louisiana Purchase in 1803 doubled the size of the United States and led Thomas Jefferson to suggest that the western territories could provide a new home for eastern Indians. The idea gained strength throughout the first three decades of the nineteenth century, with numerous events contributing to the growing support. One was the failure of the government's trading-post system. Another important factor was the continued resistance of Indian leaders and tribes to American expansion.

However, the reasons for supporting Indian removal were generally the same throughout the country. From the Ohio Valley to Georgia, Americans favored this legislation because they wanted the tribes' lands. In the North, the conflicts of the late 1700s and early 1800s, as well as the desire for land, made settlers in the region push for the relocation of the Potawatomis, Shawnees, Delawares, and Wyandots. A similar desire for land and the rise of cotton farming fueled the calls for the removal of Cherokees, Creeks, and Choctaws in the southern states.

In the late 1780s, the Shawnee, Miami, Potawatomi, and other Indian tribes in the Northwest Territory formed a military alliance against Anglo-American expansion. They wanted white settlements to stay south of the Ohio River. The councils that planned this resistance included representatives from tribes in the Great Lakes region and the Southeast. Thus, this alliance of eastern Indians was both strong and diverse.

Two different American armies suffered significant defeats in the early 1790s before General Anthony Wayne finally subdued the Indian confederates at the Battle of Fallen Timbers in 1794. The Treaty of Greenville officially ended that conflict in 1795. In this agreement, the northern Indians surrendered most of present-day Ohio. The Miami leader Little Turtle criticized American land hunger, and noted, "Your younger brothers are of the opinion you take too much of their lands away and confine the hunting of our young men with the limits too contracted."[2]

The northern Indians united again in the early 1800s. Two Shawnee Indians inspired and led this confederacy. In 1806, the Shawnee prophet Tenskwatawa began to preach against the evils of the white man's ways. He told his

Although the Battle of Tippecanoe did not bring an end to the conflict between the Indians of the Ohio Valley and the United States, it severely weakened the confederation formed by Shawnee political leader Tecumseh. This engraving depicts U.S. forces under the command of William Henry Harrison moving forward against Shawnee forces led by Tecumseh's brother Tenskwatawa during the November 7, 1811, battle.

followers to reject the material goods and Christianity of the Americans. His brother Tecumseh was the political leader of this alliance. Tecumseh traveled throughout the eastern half of the new nation to rally resistance to the intrusions of American settlers. This confederacy also suffered defeat. The most significant loss occurred in 1811, when an army under William Henry Harrison attacked and overwhelmed the Indian forces at the Battle of Tippecanoe.

However, defeat at the Battle of Tippecanoe did not end the conflict for those who had supported Tecumseh and Tenskwatawa. From 1812 through 1814, Indians in the Great Lakes region fought with the British against the Americans in the War of 1812. Indian forces contributed heavily to the capture of forts Dearborn, Mackinac, and Detroit early in the war. Despite these victories, American forces under Harrison controlled the western Great Lakes region by the beginning of 1814. Yet pockets of Indian resistance still remained in villages throughout the upper Mississippi Valley. American and British officials signed a peace treaty in December 1814, but this accord did not end the relationships between Great Lakes Indian tribes and British traders.

The end of the Indian confederacy and the War of 1812 had two results. First, military defeats led to treaties that established peace and opened lands to white settlement. By the late 1810s, thousands of settlers had flooded the Ohio Valley and lands farther west. Consequently, Ohio, Indiana, and Illinois gained statehood between 1803 and 1818. The formation of these states and the growing Anglo-American population escalated the calls to negotiate for Indian lands. By the mid-1820s, most of the Delawares and Shawnees had already signed treaties, left the Ohio Valley, and crossed the Mississippi. The Miamis, Potawatomis, Ottawas, and Wyandots who remained were under constant pressure to give up their lands. And as American expansion reached the banks of the Mississippi River, Ho-Chunk, Sauk, Mesquakie, and Menominee Indians realized that their villages were also threatened.

Another important impact of the conflicts of the early 1800s was connected to Anglo-American ideas about Indians. In part, Americans believed that the Indians' resistance to the settlement of the Ohio Valley showed that Indians would never change. Tecumseh's heroic reputation grew because he had fought nobly and did not compromise his beliefs. He had been a worthy enemy. However, after his death in 1813, he and his people became part of history. In short, many American residents of the Ohio Valley did not believe that whites and Indians could peacefully coexist. Any further conflict would only reinforce this belief. Removal, therefore, would be the best way to handle any Indians who still claimed land in the region.

The desire for land also fueled demands for removal in the Southeast. Citizens and officials of southern states attempted to obtain as much Indian territory as possible in the decades after the American Revolution. The push for land in the 1800s was directly attached to the development of cotton as a cash crop. Agriculture supported by slave labor became the core of the southern economy in the early nineteenth century. Perhaps more than any other factor, this development helps explain the widespread support for Indian removal in the region.

Many southeastern Indian tribes suffered great losses during the American Revolution. At the beginning of the conflict, few Indian leaders believed that they should side with the colonists. They realized that an American victory would lead to increased expansion west of the Appalachian Mountains. Therefore, most southeastern Indians chose between allying with the British and staying neutral. In many instances the choice did not matter. Attacks made by American militias in the first years of the war often drove neutral Indians into alliances with the British.

Indian and British forces did not fight together in the Southeast for very long. The Chickamauga Cherokees under Dragging Canoe continued to battle American militias after other Cherokees had negotiated a peace in 1777. For the most part, Indian participation in the war moved north of the Ohio River after the first two years. And once the American Revolution ended, the newly independent U.S. government focused its military efforts on the Ohio Valley. In the Southeast, federal officials chose to negotiate treaties to maintain the peace. They hoped to ensure that settlers would respect Indian boundaries.

In the decades after the American Revolution, federal officials tried to balance the land hunger of the southern states with the needs of the southeastern Indians. The southern states were the victors. Between 1798 and 1806, Cherokee leaders signed five different treaties that ceded territory in Tennessee, Georgia, Alabama, and North Carolina. Shortly thereafter, a civil war within the Creek Nation made local American citizens nervous. General Andrew Jackson eased their concerns by defeating a force of Creeks at the Battle of Horseshoe Bend in 1814. He then imposed a treaty on the entire Creek Nation that forced them to surrender about 23 million acres of land to the United States.

This 1814 treaty opened up fertile lands at a time when farmers in the South had begun to plant cotton in greater quantities than ever before. The invention of the cotton gin in 1793 had made it easier to separate seeds from cotton fibers, and the resulting increase in cotton production led to an increased reliance on African-American slave labor in the fields. But cotton quickly drained nutrients from the soil; as a result, planters always required more land. Fortunately for cotton growers, the fertile soil in Georgia and the territory that became Alabama and Mississippi was well suited to growing cotton. Established planters and hopeful settlers therefore quickly took advantage of the 1814 treaty. Between 1816 and 1820, tens of thousands of Americans entered the region. The population of Alabama alone skyrocketed from 9,046 in 1810 to 127,901 in 1820. These eager masses demanded that the U.S. government open up more land. The Creeks, Choctaws, Chickasaws, and Cherokees stood in their way.

American expansion west of the Appalachian Mountains occurred rapidly in the first decades of the nineteenth century. Indian tribes in the Great Lakes region and the South-east struggled to deal with this invasion. From the American Revolution to the 1820s, these Indians faced an inexperienced U.S. government that tried a number of policies. American officials attempted to regulate trade, contain its citizens, ne-gotiate treaties, and promote conversion to Christianity. In the end, however, all of these policies focused on obtaining Indian lands. As a result, while the conflicts over territory in the eastern half of the United States had different specific causes, the calls for removal in the 1820s were very similar.

CONCLUSION

Congress passed the Indian Removal Act in May 1830. The vote was a close one. Several congressmen spoke out pas-sionately against the legislation. Thousands of American men and women also protested this decision to make removal an official policy. However, this opposition did not change the outcome. The federal government had the authority to nego-tiate with Indians for their lands east of the Mississippi River, and treaty commissioners could arrange for Indian reloca-tion to the western territories.

Support for removal had different origins in the Old Northwest and the Southeast. The policy also had diverse impacts throughout the country. In the Southeast, the Cher-okees led the most well-known resistance to land cessions and removal, taking the fight all the way to the U.S. Supreme Court. Throughout the Old Northwest, bands of Indians struggled to hold on to small pieces of land. Although some moved by choice, most were forced to move.

One of the most famous episodes of forced removal oc-curred in the summer of 1832. From April to September of that year, a band of Sauks and Mesquakies attempted to defend their lands east of the Mississippi from the grow-ing population of American settlers in northeastern Illinois. A 65-year-old warrior named Black Hawk served as their leader and their spokesman. The resulting conflict, known as the Black Hawk War, forced the surviving Sauks and Mesquakies west of the Mississippi and secured the region for Anglo-American settlement.

By passing the Indian Removal Act, Congress made an important point clear. Decades of different government policies and conflict had led to one conclusion. The United States and its citizens had decided that American Indians did not have a place in the future of the country. Instead, Indians needed to surrender their lands and move peacefully out of the way.

The Sauk and Mesquakie in Illinois

ONLY MONTHS HAD PASSED SINCE THE END OF THE conflict known to many as the Black Hawk War. Now Black Hawk, a Sauk Indian, had decided to narrate the events in his life leading up to the 1830s. It was important to him that the American people learn why he had acted as he did in the summer of 1832. He began the story of his life with two direct statements:

> I was born at the Sac Village, on Rock river, in the year 1767, and am now in my 67th year. My great grand father, Na-nà-ma-kee, or Thunder, (according to the tradition given me by my father, Py-e-sa) was born in the vicinity of Montreal, where the Great Spirit first placed the Sac Nation, and in-spired him with a belief that, at the end of four years, he should see a *white man*, who would be to him a father.[3]

Black Hawk understood a basic but important point. The violence and misunderstandings of the summer of 1832 were rooted in numerous events of prior years. As told by Black

Hawk and noted by others of the time, the Sauk Indians had a long history with the French and British well before the American colonies gained their independence. Therefore, the relationship between the Sauk Indians and the United States was affected by decades of trade, diplomacy, and hostility.

Alternating periods of war and peace marked the Sauk Indians' dealings with the European newcomers from the 1600s to the early 1800s. But the relationship with the British had a particular impact on the ways in which the Sauks dealt with the people of the United States. Even as the young country established a strong foothold in the Ohio Valley in the first decades of the nineteenth century, Black Hawk and his people maintained a strong friendship with the British in Canada.

EARLY SAUK AND MESQUAKIE HISTORY

The Sauk Indians were relative newcomers to the upper Mississippi Valley. Indeed, Black Hawk's great-grandfather had been born near Montreal. This early history was important for two reasons. First, the westward migrations of the Sauk from the early 1600s to the 1800s reveal how they came to live in Illinois. Second, those same migrations reveal even more about their encounters with different European nations, as well as their relations with other Indian tribes.

In 1611, when the French explorer Samuel de Champlain first arrived near what became the city of Montreal, he may very well have met Black Hawk's great-grandfather. However, the Sauk Indians did not stay in the area much longer. Like other eastern Indian residents of the Great Lakes region, the Sauk were affected by the Iroquois wars. From the 1640s to the end of the century, the Five Nations of the Iroquois Confederacy engaged in extensive warfare to obtain more land west of their original homelands south of Lake Ontario and west of the Hudson River. The Iroquois were driven primarily by their desire to control the profitable beaver pelt trade between the western Indians and the French in Montreal.

Because they had depleted the animal population in their home territory in upstate New York, the Iroquois fought to obtain the harvest of furs from more bountiful lands.

This ongoing conflict gradually pushed the Sauks away from their homes on Saginaw Bay. Several decades after the arrival of the French, Sauk villages were found on Saginaw Bay in present-day eastern Michigan. More significant migrations soon followed. By the end of the seventeenth century, they had established villages throughout the region that became Illinois and Wisconsin. Safe from harassment by the Iroquois, the Sauks and their Potawatomi and Mesquakie neighbors could still trade with the Frenchmen who piloted their boats to posts at Green Bay and other western locations.

Beginning in the early 1700s, however, the relationship between the Mesquakie Indians and the French soured. The French, who referred to the Mesquakie as the Reynard, or Fox Indians, wanted to weaken Mesquakie participation in the fur trade. By the 1710s, the French joined the Huron, Ottawa, and Potawatomi tribes around Detroit in a war intended to eliminate the Mesquakie presence in the region. Although the Sauks initially allied with the French, they became upset with the Europeans' vision of total warfare. Sauk leaders feared that the elimination of the Mesquakie might lead to similar campaigns against other Indian tribes. As a result, the Sauks began to work with the Mesquakies. Warriors of these two nations fought the French and pushed south to expand their territory at the expense of the Indians in what is today Illinois.

This alliance between the Sauk and Mesquakie in the early eighteenth century had several consequences. First, the military cooperation led to villages built closer together and inter-marriage between men and women of the two communities. Second, the Sauks shared in the negative impacts of the French expeditions. As attacks by the French and their allies continued into the 1730s, the Sauks and Mesquakies moved farther west and established villages farther inland. Although they still

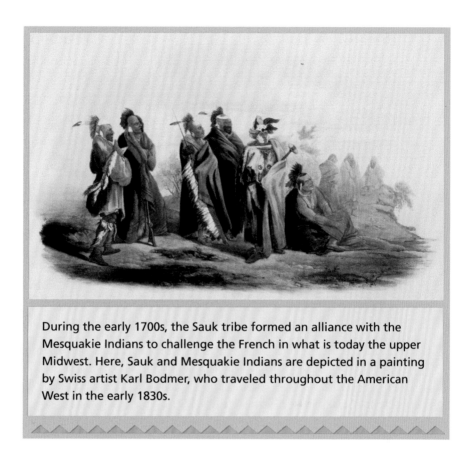

During the early 1700s, the Sauk tribe formed an alliance with the Mesquakie Indians to challenge the French in what is today the upper Midwest. Here, Sauk and Mesquakie Indians are depicted in a painting by Swiss artist Karl Bodmer, who traveled throughout the American West in the early 1830s.

traded with the Frenchmen at Green Bay, their new homes were now on the Wisconsin, Rock, and Mississippi rivers.

These years also created a foundation for misunderstandings about the relationship between the Sauks and Mesquakies. Although military alliances and intermarriage brought these two communities closer, they had their differences, too. The Sauks called themselves Osakiwugi, or the yellow earth people. The Mesquakies referred to themselves as the red earth people. Their languages were similar and they shared living styles and subsistence patterns. However, these common traits and customs did not make for a common nation.

By the end of the eighteenth century, the world of the Sauks and Mesquakies had changed dramatically. The French no longer had a significant presence in the Great Lakes region after their loss to the British in the Seven Years' War. The Sauk Indians and their neighbors at this time traveled to Green Bay and Michilimackinac to obtain goods from the British traders. Beginning in 1781, they could also trade at Prairie du Chien (in present-day Wisconsin). This friendship with the British only

WENNEBEA NAMOETA RECOUNTS SAUK HISTORY

During a journey from Chicago to Prairie du Chien in the summer of 1823, a professor from the University of Pennsylvania named William Keating spoke at length with the expedition's guide, a Sauk Indian named Wennebea Namoeta. The following excerpt is part of Keating's record of their conversations about Sauk history.

They are a brave, warlike, and, as far as we could learn, a generous people. The great reduction in their numbers arose from their hostility to the French and their allies, and also to the wars which they formerly waged against the Indians on the Missouri and Mississippi, such as the Pawnees, the Omawhaws, the Sioux, the Iowas, &c. Owing to the rapid advance of the white population, and the increasing influence of our government over them, they are becoming more peaceable, and from this circumstance their numbers are probably on the increase. Their historical recollections do not extend far back but they have been told that about sixty years since, when the French occupied the country, one of the Sauk chiefs . . . found himself surrounded with about sixty of his nation by a party of French and Indians, belonging to other tribes, amounting altogether to two thousand. Menetomet then addressed his men, bidding them not to fear, for he had been favoured with a vision from the Great Spirit that informed him that if they all grew stronger in the years after the American Revolution. Attacks by U.S militias in 1780 fostered anti-American feelings among the Indians in the region. And once the war ended between Great Britain and its former colonies, Anglo-American settlers moved into the western Great Lakes in increasing numbers.

fought bravely, not one of them should perish. Encouraged by this assertion, they fought with such desperation as to break the ranks of [missing word] and escape without the loss of a single man. . . .

Their numbers have since considerably increased, as according to his estimate, the nation now consists of upwards of a thousand warriors; in this number are included all the active, able-bodied, and middle aged part of the nation. This great accession to their numbers results principally from their system of adopting their prisoners of war. . . . The Fox nation, which appears to be very closely united with the Sauk, was at that time likewise much reduced; it is stated that at one time there were but three lodges of Fox Indians left; these reports are probably in some respects exaggerated. . . .

The Sauks have not always resided where they are at present found. Their recollection is that they formerly lived upon Saganaw Bay of Lake Huron, and that about fifty years since they removed, by the way of Greenbay, from the lake shore to their present abode. They seem to consider the name of their nation to be connected with that of Saganaw Bay, and probably derived from it. They have no account of any former migration, but entertain the opinion that the Great Spirit created them in that vicinity.*

---

* William Hypolitus Keating, comp., *Narrative of an Expedition to the Source of St. Peter's River, Lake Winnepeck, Lake of the Woods, &c. &c. Performed in the Year 1823, by Order of the Hon. J.C. Calhoun, Secretary of War, under the Command of Stephen H. Long, Major U.S.T.E.* (Philadelphia: H.C. Carey & I. Lea, 1824), 1:218–220.

THE 1804 TREATY

As mentioned earlier, in the decades after the American Revolution, the U.S. government focused its efforts on the Ohio Valley. This was most evident in the military expeditions of the 1780s and 1790s against the Indian confederacy under the Miami leader Little Turtle. But this movement into the Northwest Territory also had an impact on the lands farther west. U.S. officials knew that wars were expensive, and they did not want to fight the Sauks and their neighbors. Therefore, they tried to use peace and diplomacy to establish a presence in the Mississippi Valley.

Two important factors influenced how the Americans approached the Sauk Indians in the early nineteenth century. First, in the spring of 1803, the United States paid the French $15 million for the Louisiana Territory. This purchase doubled the size of the young nation, and at the same time it removed both the Spanish and French from the upper Mississippi Valley. The United States could now claim both sides of the river.

The second factor in the U.S. treatment of the Sauk Indians was related to this purchase. President Thomas Jefferson had a firm opinion about how the United States should use the newly acquired territory. Indeed, he believed that the western lands offered an opportunity for Indians and Americans alike. The growing U.S. population needed more land for its farms and settlements. At the same time, Indians suffered from the encroachments of settlers and the diseases and vices that came with that contact. Both populations would benefit if the Indians simply surrendered their lands and moved west.

But this vision relied on the Indians' willingness to give up their territory. Jefferson had a solution for that problem. Writing to William Henry Harrison in 1803, Jefferson outlined one part of his strategy. In an attempt to avoid wars of conquest, the United States would use trade relations to accomplish its

Upon becoming governor of Indiana Territory in 1801, William Henry Harrison attempted to obtain Indian land by enticing tribes to sign treaties. In 1804, the Sauks were tricked by Harrison into signing a treaty that made them relinquish all their lands east of the Mississippi River.

goals. "We shall push our trading houses," he explained, "and be glad to see the good and influential individuals among them [the Indians] run in debt, because we observe that when these debts get beyond what the individuals can pay, they become willing to lop them off by a cession of lands."[4] In other words, federal officials were encouraged to use whatever means necessary to convince Indian leaders to cede lands east of the Mississippi River.

Harrison, the governor of Indiana Territory from 1801 to 1813, took Jefferson's words to heart. Until 1809, Indiana Territory encompassed most of present-day Indiana, Illinois, and Wisconsin, which included the lands of the Sauks, Mesquakies, Potawatomis, and others. Harrison was a military officer who had fought against the Indian confederacy in the Ohio Valley in the 1790s. After he assumed his government post, he used councils and treaties to obtain Indian lands. In the case of the Sauks, Harrison did not deal with trade debts in an attempt to push for removal. Instead, he took advantage of conflicts between the Sauks and their white and Indian neighbors.

The Sauks had trouble deciding how they wanted to deal with U.S. officials and settlers. Hostilities during the American Revolution had inspired anti-American feelings, but the Indians did not want to anger them if it would hurt their willingness to trade. Yet the Sauks also believed that the Americans unfairly favored the Osage Indians who lived just west of the Mississippi River. The Sauks and Osages had been enemies for years, and the Sauks did not want their rivals gaining an edge in the changing world.

Sauk raiding soon led to problems with U.S. officials. In the early 1800s, the Sauks often traveled west of the Mississippi to hunt. Some of these expeditions included raids against the Osages. Attempts by federal officials to halt these attacks on the Osage villages only led to other difficulties. American settlements along the Mississippi River presented closer targets for Sauk warriors who were prevented from raiding the Osages.

In 1804, a small Sauk raiding party attacked a white settlement on the Cuivre River north of St. Louis and killed three people. These deaths had immediate consequences. Two Sauk leaders traveled to St. Louis to negotiate for peace, and while there they admitted that four of their young men had committed the murders. They offered to resolve the situation through traditional means. The Sauks would "cover the dead" by presenting gifts to the families of those who had been killed. But the settlers on Cuivre River would not accept those conditions, and federal officials demanded that the Sauks give up their young men.

To maintain the peace, the Sauk tribal council finally decided to send five minor village chiefs to St. Louis. The chiefs—Pashepaho, Quashquame, Outchequaka, Layauvois, and Hahshequarhiqua—had the authority to negotiate with U.S. officials to avoid further violence. As a sign of good faith, they also brought with them one of the young men involved in the raid. When the Sauks arrived in St. Louis, the Americans placed the young man in prison.

Because of this, the Sauk representatives viewed their mission in a new light: as both keeping the peace and gaining the release of the prisoner. They negotiated with Harrison, and the governor of Indiana Territory took advantage of the situation. He pushed the Sauk delegation to sign a treaty that made them give up some of their land. On November 3, the five men put their marks on this treaty, which surrendered all of the Sauk lands east of the Mississippi River. According to the document, the Indians were "the chiefs and head men of the united Sac and Fox tribes."[5] In this agreement, therefore, the United States granted five minor village chiefs authority over two different Indian tribes.

The true story of this treaty remains somewhat mysterious. Harrison did not keep notes of the council, and the memories of the Sauk delegation were not very detailed. Pashepaho and his colleagues would later state that they did not know what they were signing. They also argued that Harrison kept them drunk during their stay in St. Louis. Until his death, Quashquame denied that he "ever sold any land above the Rock River."[6] At the very least, it appears that Harrison used the murders of the Cuivre River settlers to advance Jefferson's goals of land cessions. The United States now had claims to most of present-day Illinois and southern Wisconsin, and the Indians no longer owned the rights to their land.

Although the 1804 treaty did not cause any immediate problems, it laid a foundation for significant conflict throughout the three decades that followed. The Sauks were angry with their delegates and confused about the actions of Harrison and the United States. Most Sauk headmen refused to recognize the validity of the treaty. However, since the agreement allowed the Sauks to remain on their lands until further notice, no major difficulties arose in 1804.

THE WAR OF 1812

The violence that did come to the Mississippi Valley in the early 1810s was not a result of the 1804 treaty. The war that broke out between the United States and Great Britain spread across the eastern half of the continent and quickly involved Indian communities throughout the Great Lakes region. The onset of war divided many Indian villages, including those of the Sauks. While a substantial number of Sauks chose to stay neutral, a larger proportion chose to join the British in their fight against the Americans. Both choices affected the future relations between the Sauks and the United States.

Even before the War of 1812 began, Harrison and other U.S. officials were concerned about Sauk and Mesquakie intentions toward the United States. By early 1810, Tecumseh and the Shawnee prophet Tenskwatawa had attracted thousands of followers to Prophetstown on the Tippecanoe River in Indiana. In the summer of 1810, federal officials believed that more than 1,000 Sauks and Mesquakies were considering joining this Indian confederacy aimed at resisting American expansion. Although parties of Sauks and Mesquakies visited Prophetstown, they never made a firm commitment to Tenskwatawa's cause.

However, there was another reason for Americans to be concerned about Sauk and Mesquakie relations with the British. Although the Indians did not join the Shawnee prophet and Tecumseh, they did often travel to Fort Malden (in present-day Ontario) in 1810 and 1811 to obtain supplies from the British agent stationed there. The British gave their visitors food, clothing, guns, and ammunition, but told the Indians to stay at peace with the Americans. That advice would soon change.

In the summer of 1812, the United States wanted to strengthen its relationship with the western Indian nations so that they would remain at peace if any conflict arose with Great Britain. But even as a delegation of 27 Sauk, Mesquakie, and Osage Indians was on its way to Washington to meet with President James Madison, the United States declared war against Great Britain. During that Washington visit and the months that followed, U.S. officials preached neutrality. The British, led by the efforts of a trader named Robert Dickson, did everything they could to get the Sauks, Mesquakies, and their neighbors involved in the war.

For Black Hawk and other Sauks, the decision to ally with the British was based in part on trade goods. Despite the promises made by President Madison and others in Washington, the American traders at Fort Madison would not supply the Indians with provisions on credit. Since the Sauks were used to receiving goods on credit in the fall and paying with the profits made from their hunts in the spring, this situation was unacceptable to them. According to messages from Dickson, the British traders were prepared to be more generous. In the wake of the Americans' unwillingness to follow through on their promises, Black Hawk became angry. "Here ended all hopes of our remaining at peace," he explained years later, "having been forced into war by being DECEIVED!"[7]

Although Black Hawk led parties of Sauk and Mesquakie men against the Americans throughout the western Great

In December 1814, the United States and Great Britain signed the Treaty of Ghent, which officially brought the War of 1812 to a close. Despite this agreement, war continued between the Sauks and the United States for another year and a half until the two sides signed a treaty in St. Louis, Missouri, in May 1816.

Lakes region, others chose to remain neutral. By the fall of 1813, about 1,500 Sauk, Mesquakie, Piankeshaw, and Iowa Indians had established villages along the Missouri River, west of St. Louis. They had crossed the Mississippi River to escape the conflict and prove to the Americans that they wanted peace.

The events of 1814 brought successes for the British and their Indian allies in the upper Mississippi Valley, but they also brought an end to the war. The Sauks and Mesquakies helped British forces defeat the Americans at a number of battles along the Mississippi River. Yet these western victories did not alter the outcome of the overall conflict. In December 1814, American and British representatives signed the Treaty of Ghent and ended the War of 1812.

The Sauks and Mesquakies found it hard to believe that the war was over. British agents had difficulty calling off war parties, and American commissioners found it hard to negotiate truces. Nearly six months after the Treaty of Ghent had been signed, Black Hawk led a raid against Fort Howard that resulted in what is known as the Battle of the Sinkhole (northwest of St. Louis). Indeed, the negotiations between the hostile Sauks and U.S. officials did not finally occur until May 1816.

CONCLUSION

The peace that was concluded with the Sauk and Mesquakie Indians at the end of the War of 1812 was important for a number of reasons. The United States negotiated with two different factions—those who lived in the villages on the Missouri River and those who had remained east of the Mississippi and allied with the British. The Missouri Sauks and Mesquakies who talked to U.S. commissioners at Portage des Sioux in 1815 signed two different treaties. Each treaty not only negotiated a truce but also confirmed the resolutions of the 1804 agreement. In their treaty, the Missouri Sauks also promised to remain separate from their relatives east of the Mississippi.

The Sauks who finally sat down with U.S. officials in St. Louis in 1816 signed a similar treaty. But Black Hawk and the other men present did not believe that they had suffered a military defeat. They recognized that the British had ended the war, but did not believe that the Americans had defeated the Indians. And despite the apparent betrayal of the Treaty of Ghent, they continued relations with the British. Indeed, Americans would refer to Black Hawk's followers as the British Band from that point forward.

Diplomacy and Conflict on the Upper Mississippi River

By 1826, WHITE SETTLERS HAD BEGUN STREAMING INTO the upper Mississippi Valley. "They say that the white people's thirst after land is so great that they are never contented until they have a belly full of it," observed Thomas Forsyth, an Indian agent, or government official put in charge of Indian affairs. "The Indians compare a white settlement in their neighborhood to a drop of raccoon's grease falling on a new blanket. The drop at first is scarcely perceptible, but in time covers almost the whole blanket."[8] At the end of the War of 1812, the Sauks and Mesquakies had not only agreed to a truce but they had also reconfirmed the resolutions of the 1804 treaty. By the mid-1820s, they were under tremendous pressure from white settlers who wanted the lands of Illinois, as well as the lead mines on the eastern banks of the Mississippi River.

For the Sauks and Mesquakies, however, the situation was further complicated by their relationships with neighboring Indian tribes. The declining wild game populations east of the Mississippi forced Sauk and Mesquakie hunters to venture farther west in search of their prey. These expeditions during the winter and summer months often led to conflicts with the Dakota Sioux bands who hunted in the same territories. Peace between these native communities was also hindered by the ambitions of young men who wanted to earn recognition as respected warriors in the tribe.

In the 1820s, then, the Sauks and Mesquakies had to concern themselves with diplomacy. The encroachment of American settlements may have created the biggest problems, especially since the white settlers knew that the 1804 treaty had granted the land to the United States. However, Sauk and Mesquakie leaders also had to deal with their Indian neighbors, even as they tried to maintain control over their younger men who wanted to prove themselves in combat. And the actions of the U.S. government had an impact on all of these relationships. U.S. officials consistently tried to maintain peaceful relations among all of the parties in the region. These attempts to hold off the violence may have led to temporary truces, but they were ultimately unsuccessful.

INTER-INDIAN RELATIONS

From 1816 forward, the United States tried to keep the peace among the various Indian tribes in the upper Mississippi Valley. To promote and protect white settlement on both sides of the Mississippi River, U.S. officials wanted to make sure that the Indians did not engage in intertribal warfare. Yet these attempts to avoid violence were seldom successful. More often than not, U.S. officials kept their own goals in mind and neglected the perspectives, desires, and traditions of the Indians. Into the mid-1820s, the Sauks and Mesquakies often found themselves more frustrated than pleased with U.S. involvement.

Throughout the early nineteenth century, Sauk and Mesquakie Indians engaged in sporadic warfare with Indians living along the Missouri River. These hostilities intensified in

By the second decade of the 1800s, wild game had begun to become depleted east of the Mississippi River. As a result, the Sauks and Mesquakies began hunting in the vicinity of the Missouri River (in present-day Missouri, Kansas, and Nebraska) and along the Des Moines River (in present-day Iowa). This led to confrontations with tribes such as the Sioux, which is depicted in this painting by American artist George Catlin.

the 1810s as the Sauks and Mesquakies sought to establish greater control over hunting territories south and west of the Missouri River; wild game populations east of the Mississippi had been steadily decreasing. Consequently, the Sauks and Mesquakies made a concerted effort to push the Osages, Otoes, Omahas, and other Missouri River tribes from their western hunting lands. This activity also led to violence with the Wahpeton and Sisseton bands of Dakota Sioux who hunted along the Des Moines River in present-day Iowa.

Government solutions to these conflicts almost always involved treaties, and this particular situation was no different. After numerous attempts to broker a peace through smaller sessions, two government officials, William Clark and Lewis Cass, called for a larger meeting. In August 1825, Clark and Cass arrived at Prairie du Chien to hold a council with nearly 2,000 Indians. Among the assembled Indians were representatives from the Sauk, Mesquakie, Menominee, Iowa, Dakota Sioux, Ho-Chunk, and the United Band of Ottawa, Ojibwa, and Potawatomi. Members of these tribes lived and hunted throughout the upper Mississippi Valley, and they needed to resolve disputes over contested land claims, boundary lines, and hunting territories.

The 1825 treaty council at Prairie du Chien was the largest gathering of Indians in the upper Mississippi Valley up to that time. Lodges of men, women, and children spread along the banks of the river for miles north and south of the settlement. The Sauks, Mesquakies, and Iowas were the last to arrive in early August, and they made a grand entrance. The men had decorated themselves as if for battle and used their arrival to demonstrate their strength and fearlessness of their enemies, particularly the Dakota Sioux. During the course of 12 days, the assembled delegates finally reached a compromise on the boundaries in question.

Although the final agreement appeared to put the intertribal problems to rest, the 1825 Treaty of Prairie du Chien did not end the conflicts. Less than five years later, the Sauks and Mesquakies registered a series of complaints with William Clark. A Sauk headman named Keokuk reported that hunting parties of the Dakota Sioux bands consistently ignored boundary lines established by the treaty resolutions. Wapello, a Mesquakie headman, made a similar criticism. "Since that time [1825] we have been much troubled about

In 1825, representatives from several Indian tribes, including Sauk, Mesquakie, Menominee, Iowa, Dakota Sioux, Ho-Chunk, and the United Band of Ottawa, Ojibwa, and Potawatomi, met at Prairie du Chien (in present-day southwestern Wisconsin) with representatives of the U.S. government. The Indian representatives who signed the resulting treaty agreed only to hunt within their tribe's designated boundary, as established by the U.S. government.

land we thought ours," he protested. "We thought the Sioux would not be allowed to hunt on our lands. . . . The Sioux do not observe the treaties they make—they violate them."[9] Once government agents realized that the Treaty of Prairie du Chien had failed to end the intertribal conflict, they called for yet another council. In 1830, the Indians of the upper Mississippi met again with the intention of finally establishing peace according to the federal government's wishes.

Three distinct issues undermined the Treaty of Prairie du Chien and threatened to weaken any further agreements. First, the boundary lines established by such treaties were never clear to everyone involved. Indeed, Clark believed that the continuing violence between the Dakota Sioux and the Sauks was a result of this misunderstanding. A second problem was more complicated and was best explained by the impact of the boundaries on the deer populations in the region. By establishing peace and separating hunting territories, the Treaty of Prairie du Chien eliminated the buffer zones between tribes that allowed the deer a relatively safe habitat. Under the new treaty, hunters could initially pursue the deer without fearing rival hunting parties. This led to overhunting and soon forced Indians to range beyond the established treaty boundaries. In other words, the solutions presented by the treaty only created more problems. It is no surprise, then, that intertribal violence in the late 1820s often began between hunting parties.

The continuous pressure applied by outsider settlement in the region created the third and final problem. As the number of Anglo-American settlers increased on the eastern side of the Mississippi River, the Sauks and Mesquakies were pushed to the western banks. To provide for their families, Indian hunters were forced to range farther from their villages and into contested territories. However, this was only one issue presented by the rising numbers of American settlers.

AMERICAN SETTLEMENT AND THE LEAD MINES

Illinois entered the Union as the twenty-first state in 1818. In 1820, it had a population of just more than 55,000, and in 1830 that population had risen to about 157,000. The explanations for this rapid population increase in the region vary. Part of the responsibility rested in federal policy. The end of the War of 1812 created a rush to settle the Great Lakes region, as many Americans established homesteads in the southern part of Illinois. But the U.S. government also promoted settlement in the region through its policy toward veterans of the war. Soldiers who had fought in the U.S. Army were given land grants of 320 acres each. They could then choose the location for their grant in sections set aside for that purpose within Arkansas, Missouri, or Illinois. The area opened to white settlement in Illinois was located between the Illinois and Mississippi rivers.

The arrival of new settlers in the southern and central portion of Illinois did not immediately affect the Sauks and Mesquakies. Their villages, fields, and livelihood were threatened more by those men who flocked to the northwestern part of the state to mine lead. The presence of lead in the area had never been a secret, and the Indians had profited from this resource for decades. But the rising demand for the element in the early nineteenth century made it increasingly valuable to the people of the United States. Thousands of Americans flooded the region between the Wisconsin and Rock rivers in the mid-to-late 1820s.

Indians had mined the lead deposits of the upper Mississippi Valley for thousands of years and used their product as a trade good well before the arrival of Europeans. Indeed, archaeologists in Alabama, Georgia, and Ontario have even unearthed beads, buttons, and pendants fashioned with lead from those mines. When the first Frenchmen floated down the Mississippi in the seventeenth century, they learned of the lead deposits and taught the local Indian populations how to smelt the ore and form it into new tools and objects. Over time this mineral resource became an important part of the Sauk and Mesquakie economy.

The presence of the French altered the importance of these lead mines among the Sauks and Mesquakies. First and foremost, the lead ore became an integral economic resource. Although Sauk and Mesquakie men continued to hunt to obtain food and furs, their trade relationship with the French in the eighteenth century included a substantial exchange in lead as well. Second, the trade with the French, and later the English, brought guns to the Indians. The presence of the lead mines and the ability to melt the ore made it easier for Sauks and Mesquakies to produce the ammunition for this welcome new technology.

The work necessary to produce the lead for trade fit in well with the traditional gender roles in Sauk and Mesquakie villages. By and large, the native women were the ones who mined the lead ore. Just as they managed the cornfields and the production of sugar, Sauk and Mesquakie women played the most important role in the production of lead. Women dug the ore from the ground, carried it to the furnaces, and smelted it. And as the demand for lead grew during the course of the eighteenth century, the women's labor became more prolonged and intensive. They produced lead for Indian and European consumers alike. "Every fall and spring hunters would go down to the mines and get a stock of bullets," a Ho-Chunk man recalled, "sometimes giving goods for it and sometimes furs."[10]

Although a number of Europeans played a part in the native production of lead, Julien Dubuque may have had the most significant impact. Dubuque was the youngest child of a well-known French-Canadian family and had moved to Prairie du Chien in 1783. He married Josette Antaya, a woman of French and Mesquakie descent. This marriage helped him establish the necessary kinship ties with the local Mesquakie community and aided his career as a trader. Perhaps most important, in 1788, the Mesquakies granted Dubuque temporary rights to a section of land on the western side of the Mississippi River that included lead mines. The Mesquakie headmen told the Frenchman that he could work that land for as long as he should live.

Dubuque lived until 1810, and during his 22 years on the Mesquakie land grant, he established a strong relationship with the local Indian populations. He not only traded in lead, but also engaged in a healthy exchange of furs and agricultural produce. Dubuque's "Mines of Spain," as he called his estate, was a center of economic and social activity in the region. It appears, however, that he actually bought more lead from local Indian women than he mined on his own property. He used his relationship with the Mesquakies to become the most prominent trader in native-mined lead in the upper Mississippi Valley. From 1788 to 1810, Sauk and Mesquakie women in the vicinity performed far more labor related to lead than they had in previous decades.

The Mines of Spain became the subject of great controversy after the trader's death. Although the Mesquakies insisted that Dubuque's land grant was temporary, others disagreed. Years before, to raise money for trade goods, Dubuque had sold the rights to a portion of his land to the St. Louis trader Auguste Chouteau. After Dubuque's death, Chouteau believed that he was the rightful owner of that section of the property. Yet the Mesquakies declared to U.S. officials that, "they never would consent to their land being sold."[11] Now there were two underlying disputes over the land in the region: The Mesquakies resisted the Chouteau claim, and both the Sauks and Mesquakies continued to contest the validity of the cessions from 1804.

Despite these issues, there were not any significant conflicts with the United States until the early 1820s, when Americans began to demand access to the lead region on the eastern side of the Mississippi River. Since the territory in question had been officially ceded in the 1804 treaty, the Americans believed that they should be allowed on those lands. Over the protests of the Sauks, Mesquakies, and Ho-Chunks, or Winnebagoes (as they were often called), whose villages were endangered by these demands, the U.S. government began to grant leases to miners. The first stage of the rush began in the summer of 1822, as several hundred miners set up camps along the Fever River in what is today northwestern Illinois and southern Wisconsin.

Thomas Forsyth, the Indian agent at the Rock River Agency in 1822, advised the Mesquakies to relocate all of their mining activities to the western side of the Mississippi River. He believed that this would be the best way to avoid conflict with the oncoming American miners. Mesquakie leaders hoped to compromise and offered to lease their lands for a period of four years. Forsyth and the United States refused this offer, and instead told the Indians that any physical resistance would result in U.S. military intervention.

From 1822 to 1828, in what is today northwestern Illinois and southern Wisconsin, tensions began to rise. The lead mining district, the center of all the activity during those years, lay south of the Wisconsin River and north of the Rock River. The non-Indian population of that region was only about 200 in 1825, but it had risen to more than 4,000 by 1827. Nearly all of these miners were young white men, eager to earn their fortune and ready to take on anyone who stood in their way.

The needs and desires of the miners clashed with those of the Sauks, Mesquakies, and Ho-Chunks. Miners often trespassed on Indian lands, and native headmen did what they could to expel the intruders without igniting a conflict. Local Indian agents also received complaints of harassment, particularly involving male miners and native women. The situation was tense, but substantial trouble was often avoided. Although there was little violence between Indians and miners from 1822 to 1826, that situation soon changed.

On June 24, 1827, members of the Prairie La Crosse band of Ho-Chunks attacked the home of the Gagnier family, north of Prairie du Chien. The Indians were retaliating, in part, for the continued intrusions of American miners on their lands. This Winnebago revolt, as it is known, was short lived. The next and final incident involved an assault on two small boats carrying American miners. In the end, few Indians in the region joined in the uprising and a quick show of force by the U.S. Army convinced any doubters that resistance would not be wise.

Yet the Ho-Chunk attacks revealed the anger of the native residents of the lead mining district. They were upset with the continued invasion of the miners and they could not believe that the U.S. government would not take action. Carumna, a Ho-Chunk chief, told Joseph Street that the Indians had not expected this invasion. "The hills are covered with them," the headman informed the Indian agent. "More are coming, and shoving us off our lands to make lead. We want our Father [President John Quincy Adams] to stop this before blood may be shed by bad men."[12]

INCURSIONS ON HO-CHUNK LAND

In November 1827, Joseph M. Street assumed his new position at the head of the Winnebago Indian Agency at Prairie du Chien. At this time, tensions were rising because of the encroachment of American settlers on Ho-Chunk, or Winnebago, lands in the lead mining region. The following excerpts come from a letter that Street wrote to Governor Ninian Edwards of Illinois.

The Indians had been soured by the conduct of the vast number of adventurers flocking to and working the lead mines of Fever River. Those who went by land, by far the greater part, passed through the Winnebago country. Many of them had great contempt for "naked Indians," and behaved low, gross, and like blackguards amongst them. The Agent at the mines granted permits on the Winnebago lands, and numerous diggings were industriously pushed far east of the line between the Ottawas, Chippewas and Pottawatomies of the Illinois, and the Winnebagoes, and great quantities of mineral procured and taken away to the smelters. . . .

I should first have called your attention to your treaty of the 24 Aug., 1816, and the treaty of 19 Aug., 1825, which together establish

Carumna's words fell on deaf ears. By the late 1820s, the protests of Ho-Chunk, Sauk, and Mesquakie leaders would not be able to halt the encroachments of American settlers in the region. Just as important, those protests would fail to persuade government officials that something needed to be done about it. Joseph Street, Thomas Forsyth, William Clark, and other federal agents in the region believed that the time had come for the Indians to leave their lands on the eastern side of the Mississippi River. These men appeared more than willing to enforce the terms of the 1804 treaty.

the line between the Ottawas, etc., and the Winnebagoes . . . From this you perceive that you in the treaty of 24 Aug., 1816 made the only reservations that have been made, and they are all west of the line of the Winnebagoes. Then we have no colour of claim on the Winnebago lands whatever. Harrison indeed bought all this land by the treaty of 3d Nov., 1804, from a point 36 miles up the Wisconsin to Lake Sakaegan, at the head of Fox River of the Illinois. This includes the whole mining district, 80 or a hundred miles east of the mouth of Fever River. But in the treaty of the 19th Aug., 1825, the commissioners recognize and establish the right of the Winnebagoes to this land, and make no exception or reservation except at P. du Ch. This closes all our chance of claim. This is the treaty you said you had never noticed, and that you would have opposed its ratification had you considered its provisions. The Winnebagoes complained of the trespass of the miners, and the open violation of the treaty by the permits of Mr. Thomas, the Ag't. No notice was taken and the diggings progressed. The Indians attempted force which was repelled, and very angry feelings produced.*

* Joseph Montfort Street, "Letters about White Incursions onto Indian Lands in 1827," Wisconsin Historical Society. Available online at *http://www.wisconsin history.org/turningpoints/search.asp?id=265.*

CONCLUSION

The Sauk and Mesquakie were only two of the many Indian nations inhabiting the upper Mississippi Valley in the late 1700s and early 1800s. Villages housing thousands of men, women, and children rested along the banks of the rivers throughout the region. The hunting practices of these native populations, as well as the ambitions of young men within each tribe, often made it difficult to maintain the peace. And in the first two decades of the nineteenth century, the situation became even more complicated with the arrival of thousands of American settlers who sought land and the resources that the land contained. It was a potentially volatile mix if not managed well.

In the 1820s, the U.S. government and its agents illustrated that it either could not or would not handle the challenge presented by the populations in that region. American attempts to mediate peaceful relations among the Indians were ultimately unsuccessful, in part because federal officials did not appear to understand the problem. The efforts to maintain peace between the miners and the Indians failed for another reason entirely. As demonstrated by the leases given to miners and the advice given to Indians, U.S. officials in the late 1820s had made two critical decisions. They would allow miners access to the lead, and either encourage or force the Indians to move west of the Mississippi River.

Sauk Leadership Fragments

In the late 1820s, the leadership of the Sauk Indians was disjoined. "We were a divided people," Black Hawk noted, "forming two parties. Ke-o-kuck being at the head of one, willing to barter our rights merely for the good opinion of the whites; and cowardly enough to desert our village to them. I was at the head of the other party, and was determined to hold on to my village, although I had been ordered to leave it."[13] His description fit the general understanding of most U.S. officials at the time. As far as the federal government was concerned, Keokuk was the headman who had the realistic and proper view of the situation. He agreed that it was useless and wrong to resist, and that it would be best for the Sauks if they negotiated with the Americans and moved west of the Mississippi River. Black Hawk, on the other hand, was viewed as the troublemaker. He was the man who refused to listen to the reasoning of the government and refused to surrender the tribe's ancestral village of Saukenuk.

Although Keokuk and Black Hawk are two of the most in-fluential and prominent Sauk Indians of that era, their story and their differences are not so clear-cut. Both men rose to positions of leadership outside of the traditional channels. In some respects, they should not have been the headmen of the two sides within their nation. Yet the circumstances of the time created the opportunity for each man to exert a tremendous amount of influence.

From 1828 to 1831, the Sauks confronted a U.S. government intent on relocating them west of the Mississippi River. The members of the Sauk Nation had two different paths they could follow: that of Keokuk, or that of Black Hawk. Keokuk preached peace, negotiation, and relocation. Black Hawk argued that the Sauks could not and should not abandon Saukenuk in the face of American pressure and deceit. Neither position was necessarily better than the other; however, these differing stances meant that by the summer of 1831, the Mississippi River divided the settlements of the Sauks and Mesquakies.

TRADITIONS OF SAUK LEADERSHIP

Leadership among the Sauk Indians was structured by a variety of societal divisions and traditions. A tribal council, which included representatives from each of the 12 clans, oversaw affairs for the entire nation. The council did not have the authority to impose its will on its people and relied to a great extent on persuasion and social pressure. Strong headmen had to have the respect of their people to maintain a position of influence. In addition to this more formal structure, the Sauks also had more localized leaders in their villages. However, the most influential men of the different settlements were not necessarily the men who sat in the tribal council.

Positions of leadership were hereditary through the clans. The Trout and Sturgeon clans provided the civil chiefs, while the Fox clan provided the war chiefs. Yet this was not the only level of social organization. At birth, Sauk boys were placed in one of two groups within the tribe, the Kishkoa and the

Oshkash. The first male child followed his father's lineage, and the second son became a member of the other division. In part, these two social divisions organized the Sauk tribe for internal competitions, where the Kishkoa would cover themselves in white clay and the Oshkash in black charcoal. This in turn trained the young men for the future roles in their community.

The Sauk tribal council was in charge of treaty negotiations and other meetings with Indian delegations and U.S. officials. Although this council oversaw most social and political matters, it did not direct all tribal affairs. When it came to raids on other Indian tribes and decisions to go to war, the tribal council had less control. Such decisions were left to the Sauk men who had earned reputations as successful leaders. Indeed, any individual could raise a war party under the right circumstances.

Because of the events of the late eighteenth and early nineteenth centuries, successful war leaders gained more influence within Sauk society. Those decades witnessed a significant amount of violence both between Indian tribes themselves and between Indians and U.S. citizens. The Indian men who showed bravery during those times and led their people to victories earned respect and influence beyond their station. The tribal council did not disappear during those years, but the most authoritative voices within the councils had changed.

The Sauks experienced this transition just as strong leadership had become so crucial. In the first three decades of the nineteenth century, and especially in the 1820s, the relationship with the U.S. government depended on the abilities of Sauk headmen to negotiate with federal officials. It was not just a question of who the Sauks wanted to represent them, but with whom the U.S. officials would negotiate in council. This circumstance made the differences between Black Hawk and Keokuk even more apparent and important.

At the time of this early 1830s oil painting by George Catlin, Black Hawk, or Makataimeshekiakiak, would have been in his mid-60s. Although he never rose to the status of chief, Black Hawk was a prominent warrior who gained notoriety because he refused to abandon traditional Sauk ways.

BLACK HAWK AND TRADITION

Makataimeshekiakiak, or Black Hawk, was not a principal chief of the Sauks. He was 63 years old in 1830 and one of the elders of his people. His voice was heard in councils and U.S. officials knew his name, but he had earned a position among the leading men as a warrior, not as a diplomat or a civil chief.

Black Hawk's first notable exploit as a warrior came at the age of 15, when he killed an enemy in battle for the first time. He and his father, Pyesa, had joined a Sauk war party against the Osage, and the young Black Hawk took the scalp of an Osage warrior. Upon his return to Saukenuk, Black Hawk participated in a scalp dance for the first time and began his rise to glory. He led a successful raid several months later and gained further acclaim. Before he had reached the end of his second decade, he had already led 200 men against the Osage settlements west of the Mississippi River.

In his early 20s, Black Hawk lost his father and inherited an important emblem of the Sauks. Pyesa died in a battle against the Cherokees and his son could not save his father's life. "I now fell heir to the great medicine bag of my forefathers, which had belonged to my father,"[14] Black Hawk reported. The young man viewed this bag with reverence and a sense of duty. Within this bundle made of either animal skin or birch bark, Black Hawk held amulets that were both the keys to military success and, in his words, "the soul of the Sac nation."[15] He did not bear this burden lightly.

Although his lineage and possession of this medicine bag granted Black Hawk substantial respect within the Sauk community, it was his continued martial exploits that earned him a place at their councils. He continued to lead war parties against their enemies and actively supported the British against the Americans in the War of 1812. At the war's end, he reluctantly signed a peace treaty that confirmed the resolutions of the 1804 accord.

The treaty he signed in 1816 is important for another reason. The leaders and prominent men of the Sauks at Rock River signed this treaty, and Black Hawk's name was only eighth on the list. He was nearly 50 years old and a reputable warrior, but he was not the leader of the Sauks at Rock

River. Similarly, when 10 Sauk and Mesquakie chiefs traveled to Washington, D.C., in 1824 to negotiate a peace with the Dakota Sioux, Black Hawk did not go. His authority did not extend past leadership on raids.

Nevertheless, by the late 1820s, Black Hawk had become a prominent voice because he refused to give up traditional ways. He had spent his life as a warrior, leading Sauk men against their enemies. Despite the outcome of the War of 1812, he continued to travel to Canada to trade and talk with the British. He had lived for more than 60 years according to the principles of Sauk society and traditions, and expected to continue his

THE MEDICINE BAG

Throughout his autobiography, Black Hawk talks about the medicine bag of the Sauks that he inherited from his father. He carried this bag throughout his life and viewed it with great reverence. In the excerpt below, a Sauk Indian named Wennebea Namoeta describes the importance of the medicine bag to the Sauks.

"You know," said he, "that we always carry medicine bags about us, and that in these we place the highest confidence; that we take them when we go to war; that we administer of their contents to our relations when sick, &c. The great veneration in which we hold them, arises from our deeming them indispensable to obtain success against our enemies. They have been transmitted to us by our forefathers, who received them at the hands of the Great Master of Life himself. We never venture upon a warlike undertaking unless, by their means, our chiefs should have previously had visions, advising them rode so. When we are near to our enemies, they impart to us the faculty of beholding, in the heavens, great fires passing from one cloud to another. If these fires be numerous, long-continued, and extensive, it is a sure sign to seasonal rounds despite the pressures of the world around him. Most important, he believed that the Sauks and Mesquakies had been deceived several times over and that they had never surrendered their homelands to the Americans.

KEOKUK AND THE POLITICS OF ACCOMMODATION

Keokuk became the foil to Black Hawk in many respects. He was younger than Black Hawk by a little more than a decade, born into the Fox clan and therefore a warrior by birth. Unlike Black Hawk, however, Keokuk gained a position of

us that in the part of the heavens where we behold them, there are enemies; that they are powerful and numerous, and that we must avoid them. If, on the contrary, they be few, faint and not frequent, then it is a token that our enemies are weak, and that we may attack them with a certainty of success. These are not visions, but realities; we do not dream that we see these fires, but we actually behold them in the heavens; for this reason do we value our medicine bags so highly that we would not part with them while life endures. True, some of us did, at one time, at the instigation of the Shawanese prophet [Tecumseh's brother], throw them away, but this proved to us the source of many heavy calamities, it brought on the death of all who parted with their bags. To this cause do we attribute the great mortality which we experienced, during the late war against the Americans. He [the Shawanese prophet] came to us, and by artifice induced us to throw away our medicine, a circumstance which we have since had cause to regret.*

* William Hypolitus Keating, comp., *Narrative of an Expedition to the Source of St. Peter's River, Lake Winnepeck, Lake of the Woods, &c. &c. Performed in the Year 1823, By Order of the Hon. J.C. Calhoun, Secretary of War, Under the Command of Stephen H. Long, Major U.S.T.E.* (Philadelphia: H.C. Carey & I. Lea, 1824), 1:229–231.

influence because of the battles he did not fight—he preferred peaceful negotiation to bloodshed. U.S. officials respected his eloquence and granted him power because he was willing to negotiate. And while Black Hawk assumed a stance in direct opposition to the Americans, Keokuk worked with the U.S. government to keep his people safe from harm. However, Keokuk had not always favored capitulation. He rose to prominence during the War of 1812, when his eloquence and courage earned him a position in the tribal council.

In October 1813, the residents of Saukenuk received word that an American force was headed in their direction. With many of their warriors absent, the Sauk leadership decided to temporarily relocate across the river. Keokuk was 33 years old and not allowed to be present at the council. Yet when he heard of the decision, he asked permission to speak. He criticized the principal men for their cowardice and declared that he would stand and fight. The Sauk council took courage from his stance and gave him their support. Although the American attack did not materialize, Keokuk had now earned a new position as war chief for Saukenuk.

The next significant transition in Keokuk's status occurred in the early 1820s, as American settlers began to move into northwestern Illinois. Most notably, Keokuk became a well-liked figure among federal officials in the region. Both Thomas Forsyth at the Rock River Agency and William Clark in St. Louis began to see Keokuk as a capable and friendly negotiator. They believed that they could rely on him to keep the peace, and they gradually gave him more authority over the distribution of Sauk annuities. Control over these goods further increased Keokuk's influence among his people. And while Black Hawk stayed home, Keokuk made the journey to Washington with nine other Sauk and Mesquakie leaders in 1824. In Washington, the young Sauk leader was able to convince Secretary of War John C. Calhoun that the Sauks had never ceded any territory west of the Mississippi River.

Unlike Black Hawk, Keokuk advocated accommodation and believed that the Sauks should move west from their traditional homeland. As a result of Keokuk's conciliatory stance, the U.S. government recognized him as the true leader of the Sauks.

During meetings with U.S. officials in 1824 and the years that followed, however, Keokuk did not dispute the cessions of Sauk and Mesquakie territory east of the Mississippi River. He wanted to work with the Americans to ensure a better place for his people. He also did not relinquish his position as a warrior and led parties against both the Dakota Sioux and the Menominees in the 1820s. As late as 1831, he asserted the need for the U.S. government to stop meddling in Indian affairs. "Why do you not let us be as the great Spirit made us," he argued, "and let us settle our own difficulties?"[16] But as long as he was able to protect the Sauk lands west of the Mississippi River, he was not going to fight the resolutions of the 1804 treaty. In this, Keokuk and Black Hawk would never see eye to eye.

SAUKENUK AND DEBATES OVER RELOCATION

Black Hawk's and Keokuk's differing perspectives on Sauke-nuk and the retention of villages on the eastern side of the Mississippi River best illustrate their opposing views. Black Hawk refused to consider a permanent relocation to the western territories if it meant surrendering their main vil-lage on the Rock River. And he had nothing but contempt for Keokuk's attempts to convince the residents of Saukenuk to abandon their homes. "I looked upon him [Keokuk] as a coward, and no brave," Black Hawk asserted, "to abandon his village to be occupied by strangers."[17]

The village of Saukenuk held a special place in Black Hawk's life. It was the site of his birth and it was the center of the Sauk world. Its lodges held several thousand Sauks in the early 1800s, and they benefited from the rich environment of the region. The women of the village tended nearly 800 acres of fields that included corn, beans, and squash. The fish from the Rock River provided further sustenance. The men would hunt on the western prairies in the summer months and return for the harvest in the fall, and during the winter, the Sauks would leave their village and spend the next several months in smaller hunting groups. Then when the ground thawed and winter waned, they would return to their village on the Rock River and begin their cycle anew.

From 1828 to 1831, events in the region severely disrupted that cycle and created problems both within the Sauk Nation and between the Sauks and the Americans. In June 1828, Thomas Forsyth talked to Sauk and Mesquakie leaders at Rock Island. His main intention was to convince the Indians that they needed to permanently relocate their villages to the western side of the Mississippi River. The number of American settlements was on the rise and the river traffic between St. Louis and the lead mines north of Saukenuk would continue to intrude on the livelihood of the Indian residents. The Sauks and Mesquakies refused to consider this proposition.

The struggle over Saukenuk began that winter. While the Sauks were on their winter hunt, three white families entered the village and occupied what they viewed as abandoned lodges. The Sauks learned of this, and Black Hawk left the hunt to investigate. He returned to find one of the families living in his own home. Although he traveled to Rock River and Prairie du Chien to complain about the situation, no federal official would force the squatters to leave the village. When winter came to a close, the Sauks could not agree whether or not they should return to Saukenuk.

Black Hawk and several hundred Sauks insisted on returning to their homes. Keokuk traveled with them, but only so he could either try to reach a compromise with the Americans or convince his people to abandon Saukenuk. He was not successful, and the Sauk women did what they could to plant crops in the areas left unclaimed by the squatters. The rest of the year passed without any notable incidents, though both Keokuk and federal agents repeatedly informed the Indian residents of Saukenuk that they would have to leave in time.

The relative peace did not slow down the push for removal. As the Sauks prepared for their winter hunt in the fall of 1829, Forsyth gave them some unwelcome news. Beginning in late October, the land in and around Saukenuk would go on sale. In accordance with the terms of the 1804 treaty, each sale would confirm that the land no longer belonged to the Sauks.

Nevertheless, Black Hawk and a significant number of Sauks continued to believe that they could and should live at Saukenuk. In the spring of 1830, they returned and broke ground on the sections of land that had not been sold the previous fall. Unsuccessful hunts had made for a tough winter, and the American settlers at Saukenuk further hindered the Indians' ability to obtain the necessities of life. However, the Sauks refused to concede to the wishes of all who told them to leave.

During the course of 1830, Black Hawk traveled throughout the Great Lakes region seeking advice. He spoke to British officials at Fort Malden, who stated that he needed to talk to U.S. president Andrew Jackson, and that Jackson would deal with the Indians fairly. The Sauk leader also consulted Lewis Cass, then the governor of Michigan Territory, who informed him that if the Sauks had not sold the land and remained at peace, they would not have been disturbed. Finally Black Hawk spoke to Wabokieshiek, or White Cloud, the Ho-Chunk prophet whose village was about 30 miles northeast of Saukenuk on the Rock River. Wabokieshiek supported Black Hawk's stance and agreed that the Sauks and Mesquakies had not ceded their lands.

Even as Black Hawk journeyed to gain support for his people, other events created problems. In May 1830, Congress passed the Indian Removal Act and granted authority to federal officials to arrange for the relocation of Indians to the western territories. Earlier that same month, a war party of Dakota Sioux, Ho-Chunks, and Menominees attacked an unarmed diplomatic delegation of Mesquakie village leaders. Only one Mesquakie survived, and news of the attack created an uproar throughout the upper Mississippi Valley. The Mesquakies blamed the American agent who had arranged for a council and they called for revenge. Federal officials did what they could to preserve the peace, but the Mesquakies wanted war.

White Cloud, or Wabokieshiek, was a Ho-Chunk prophet who advised Black Hawk and supported his opposition of the U.S. government. White Cloud is depicted here in this 1832 portrait by George Catlin.

From the fall of 1830 to the summer of 1831, the mood in the region was tense. The threat of intertribal warfare made the citizens of Illinois nervous and heightened the calls for Indian removal. Mesquakie warriors continued to seek revenge even as Sauk and Mesquakie leaders called for peace. Black Hawk gained an increasing number of followers, as he stood firm in his position to return to Saukenuk once more. War would not begin in 1831, but the events of that year laid the foundation for the conflict that broke out the following summer.

CONCLUSION

Leadership among the Sauk Indians was based on influence rather than absolute authority. It was at once a source of strength and a point of conflict when dealing with U.S. officials. And it also meant that there was more than one path to leadership. This was illustrated very well in the first three decades of the nineteenth century. Neither Black Hawk nor Keokuk was a hereditary chief within Sauk traditions. Nevertheless, they both became identified inside and outside the nation as the men who spoke for the different factions of the Sauk.

By the summer of 1831, Keokuk and Black Hawk clearly represented two different courses of action. Keokuk was the man with whom the U.S. government wanted to negotiate. Councils with this Sauk leader created compromise, and by the summer of 1829, he had established his village on the banks of the Iowa River, west of the Mississippi. He represented the peaceful pro-removal Indian that Americans favored. Black Hawk, on the other hand, was the symbol of discontent and an apparent magnet for like-minded Sauks and Mesquakies. He refused to surrender Saukenuk and abandon tradition. By the summer of 1831, therefore, his band and Saukenuk became the focal point for both Indian resistance and Indian removal in the upper Mississippi Valley.

The Onset of War

THERE IS SOME DISAGREEMENT AMONG HISTORIANS over when and how the event known as the Black Hawk War began. Some might argue that the conflict began as soon as Black Hawk and more than 1,000 Sauks and Mesquakies crossed the Mississippi River and journeyed toward their former home on the Rock River. Others might claim that the responsibility for the violence rests on the shoulders of the anxious Illinois militiamen who fired on a small party of Sauks bearing a white flag of truce.

To some extent, both are correct. Because of the sequence of events leading up to the summer of 1832, conflict between Black Hawk's band and the citizens of Illinois was nearly un-avoidable. Black Hawk firmly believed two things: First, that the Sauks and Mesquakies had never ceded their lands east of the Mississippi. Second, that the village of Saukenuk was too important to give up and would be abandoned only by force. "It was here that I was born," he explained, "and here lie the bones of many friends and relations. For this spot I felt a sacred reverence, and could never consent to leave it, without being forced therefrom."[18] The citizens and politicians of Illinois held similarly strong beliefs. They relied on the treaty of 1804 to assert their claim to the former Sauk and Mesquakie land and to confirm that these Indians no longer had any valid claim to that territory. They also believed that Black Hawk could not be trusted and was usually up to no good.

Sauk and Mesquakie headmen, as well as federal officials, pleaded for peace and repeatedly told Black Hawk and his followers to stay west of the Mississippi. The elderly Sauk warrior did not intend to antagonize, but he also refused to back down. He was not alone. The men and women who traveled with Black Hawk held similarly strong beliefs about the need for their people to return to and retain Saukenuk. But the passion of their beliefs was taken for stubborn resistance, and their return to Illinois was seen as a sign of aggression. The beginning of the conflict, therefore, cannot be blamed on any single event. The violence of 1832 was simply the result of decades of misunderstandings and a stubborn refusal on both sides to surrender their positions.

CROSSING THE MISSISSIPPI RIVER IN 1831

In the spring of 1831, Black Hawk and a large number of Sauks and Mesquakies crossed the Mississippi River with the intention of reclaiming their homes and fields at Saukenuk. On the one hand, this move was part of an annual cycle. It was time to plant corn after a long winter west of the Mississippi. On the other hand, it was a risky act of determination on the part of Black Hawk and the British Band. By 1831, the citizens and politicians of Illinois wanted to force the Indians to stay on the western side of the river. Indeed, conflict was narrowly avoided in 1831, when federal and state officials moved quickly to remove the Indians from Illinois.

Despite the pleas of Keokuk and other Sauk and Mesquakie leaders, Black Hawk led the British Band from their western hunting grounds to Saukenuk in the spring of 1831.

Even though so many voices were raised against him and his actions, Black Hawk was not troubled. "I had one consolation," he reflected, "for all the women were on my side, on account of their corn-fields."[19] It was an important point. Black Hawk's words and actions are often believed to be responsible for the events of these fateful years. Yet his followers were just as adamantly in support of his views. The women who had so long been responsible for the cornfields of Saukenuk were just as attached to the land as the men who led them. Thus the return to the eastern side of the Mississippi River was the result of communal interest, not the ambitions of a single individual.

Upon their arrival at Saukenuk, the Indians first had to deal with the families of squatters who had taken over their lodges and fields. The appearance of this band of Indians may have taken the settlers by surprise, for most left the day after Black Hawk and the other leaders told them that they should. Within a few days of their arrival, the Sauks and Mesquakies were settling in at Saukenuk. The women began to prepare the fields for planting, and the men set about making the lodges habitable.

But this return to Saukenuk was not without opposition. Although the women began to plant corn, the remaining squatters undermined those efforts by plowing over the newly planted fields. More important, Illinois officials reacted quickly to what they saw as an invasion. Governor John Reynolds issued a call to organize a state militia to remove the Indians from the state. Major General Edmund Gaines, who was the commander of the U.S. Army's Western Department, told Reynolds that such a move was unnecessary. Instead, Gaines ordered six companies of infantry to march north to Rock River.

Word traveled fast, and the Sauks and Mesquakies at Saukenuk heard of the impending arrival of the U.S. soldiers at the beginning of June. As he had done so many times before, Black Hawk consulted with Wabokieshiek. The Ho-Chunk leader told him that as long as the Sauks and

Like Black Hawk, Mesquakie chief Wapello signed the "Articles of Agreement and Capitulation" in 1831, which ceded Sauk and Mesquakie land east of the Mississippi River to the U.S. government. Wapello is depicted here by American artist Charles Bird King, who catalogued the tribes of the United States in a three-volume work.

Mesquakies remained at peace, the United States would not force them from the land. Such advice helped to keep the peace, but it was not the reality of the situation.

Gaines used his show of force to bring the Indians to council. The first session opened on the morning of June 5.

Black Hawk was not there, but Keokuk was, as was the Mesquakie leader Wapello. Gaines wanted these two men at the council to persuade their relatives to remove peacefully to the villages on the western side of the Mississippi River. Before anyone could officially open the meeting, however, Black Hawk and his followers arrived. They were singing a war song and were armed for battle. According to Black Hawk, they intended to show Gaines that they were not afraid.

Gaines refused to be intimidated and confronted Black Hawk. When the Sauk warrior refused to concede that his people had sold their lands, Gaines engaged in a shouting match with him. The general looked around at the assembled Indians, most of whom were the established civil leaders of the Sauk and Mesquakie nations, and questioned the war leader's presence at the council. "Who is *Black Hawk*?" Gaines shouted angrily. Black Hawk was quick to respond. "I am a *Sac*! My forefather was a SAC! And all the nations call me a SAC!"[20]

The strength of Black Hawk's response did not deter Gaines from delivering his message. He had brought the soldiers to move the Indians back across the Mississippi, and he was willing and ready to use force if necessary. Despite his belligerence in council, Black Hawk did not want to be reckless with the lives of his followers. When Gaines refused their request to remain at Saukenuk until they could harvest their corn, the Sauks and Mesquakies took action to avoid potential conflict. On the night of June 25, Black Hawk and the members of the British Band left Saukenuk and crossed the Mississippi River under the cover of darkness.

Although the removal was complete, Gaines had further business to accomplish. On June 30, he sat in council with the Sauk and Mesquakie leadership, including Black Hawk and other members of the British Band. At the end of this council, everyone, including Black Hawk, placed their marks on a document titled "Articles of Agreement and Capitulation." The terms were clear. From that day forward, the British Band would submit to the authority of Keokuk and the other civil chiefs. They would also sever all ties to the British traders and officials in Canada. And once again, the Sauks and Mesquakies were forced to confirm the validity of the 1804 treaty and the agreements that followed.

The articles written up by Gaines and Reynolds were supposed to reinforce everything that had been said and done in the preceding months. Even Black Hawk noted that he intended to live in peace under this treaty. He and his followers set up homes in present-day Iowa. Black Hawk requested a small log cabin and agricultural assistance from the federal government. He was 65 years old and it appeared that both the might of the United States and the expansion of its settlements now compelled him to accept the loss of his former lands.

CROSSING THE MISSISSIPPI RIVER IN 1832

In the spring of 1832, however, Black Hawk once again crossed the Mississippi River. Despite the events of the previous year, including the negotiations with Gaines, the Sauk leader refused to stay in Iowa. Once again he did not travel alone, and once again his return produced a strong reaction from the citizens of Illinois. This time, conflict could not be avoided.

Several circumstances led to Black Hawk's return. The first of these events began with a message brought to Black Hawk by Neapope, the only member of the British Band who was also a regular member of the Sauk tribal council. Neapope was only 28 years old, and his youth reflected the new leadership of the British Band. At the end of the summer of 1831, both the Sauk leader Bad Thunder and the Mesquakie headman Morgan had died, leaving younger men to take their place. Neapope was one of those men.

The young Sauk had traveled to visit the British at Fort Malden and was not present when General Gaines forced Black Hawk and the British Band back into Iowa. U.S. authorities were not aware of Neapope's journey, and when he returned in the fall of 1831, he stopped first at the prophet Wabokieshiek's village. After spending the winter there, he went to see Black Hawk in Iowa. At that time, Neapope told the old Sauk warrior two important pieces of information: First, the British would support the Sauks if they returned to Saukenuk in the spring. Second, Wabokieshiek had invited Black Hawk and his people to live at his village on the Rock River and plant corn.

Neapope's message reignited the spark that had been smothered by the negotiations with Gaines the previous summer. Black Hawk gathered the Sauks and Mesquakies together to tell them the news. Keokuk's position was clear. According to Black Hawk, the Sauk headman argued "that I had been imposed upon by *liars* and had much better remain where I was and keep quiet."[21] In hindsight this was good advice, but at the time, Black Hawk refused to listen to a man he deemed a coward.

Other circumstances also fueled the Sauks' desire to cross the Mississippi and their willingness to believe in the possibility of British support. Because they left Saukenuk in the summer of 1831, before they could harvest any corn, the Sauks were dependent on the U.S. government for much-needed supplies. Unfortunately, by late winter those provisions had begun to run out and the Sauks who lived in Iowa were in trouble. Rumors had also spread that U.S. citizens and soldiers were disrupting Indian graves at Saukenuk. When small parties of Sauk men crossed the river to rebury the dead and perhaps get some corn, they were driven off by armed militiamen and citizens.

By April 1832, then, a series of events had created an environment in which Black Hawk and a mixed band of Sauks and Mesquakies felt that a return to Saukenuk was justified and necessary. It appeared that the British in Canada would send supplies to support the move, and a return to their eastern lands would be the only way to provide for their families and protect their ancestors. Even if they could not settle at Saukenuk, they could accept Wabokieshiek's invitation to

A veteran of the War of 1812, Major General Edmund Gaines commanded the U.S. Army's Western Department during the Black Hawk War of 1832. Although he was instrumental in forcing Black Hawk to leave Illinois in 1831, Gaines and the U.S. Army would have to deal with Black Hawk again the following year.

live at his village. Keokuk and other civil leaders continued to protest their actions, but their words had no effect.

The British Band were making their own decisions now, and the Indians who belonged to this community did not listen to the Sauk and Mesquakie headmen who remained in Iowa. Neapope and seven other men represented the civil leadership of this loosely organized band, and Black Hawk was recognized as one of five war chiefs. Black Hawk was the eldest of these chiefs, and therefore had the respect of all, but he was not the only leader. In the spring of 1832, this band also included about 100 Kickapoo Indians who wanted to return to Illinois. Once they crossed the river, another 100 Ho-Chunks under Wabokieshiek joined as well.

The actual crossing occurred on April 6, 1832, at a spot more than 60 miles south of Saukenuk. Estimates of the number of Indians in the group vary, but the band included at least 500 warriors and several hundred additional men, women, and children. Without hesitation, they began to head north along the banks of the Mississippi. "Our women and children in canoes, carrying such provisions as we had, camp equipage, &c., and my braves and warriors on horseback, armed and equipped for defence,"[22] Black Hawk recalled. The band moved forward with determination and prepared for what lay ahead.

MISUNDERSTANDINGS AND THE BATTLE OF STILLMAN'S RUN

The river crossing brought a number of responses from federal and state officials, and few Americans believed that the Indians' intentions could be anything but hostile. However, it was a series of misunderstandings that led to the first gunshots. In the end, the heightened tensions, built upon attitudes and events of previous years, made it nearly impossible to avoid a struggle.

U.S. soldiers were already on the move in early April, but their movement had nothing to do with Black Hawk. Instead, their primary mission was to prevent war between the Menominees and the Mesquakies. During the previous spring, a war party of Mesquakies had killed 29 Menominees in response to the death of their unarmed chiefs in May 1830. Now the Menominees were threatening to take revenge and

Brigadier General Henry Atkinson had been charged with keeping the peace. As Atkinson and more than 200 soldiers traveled up the Mississippi River toward Prairie du Chien via steamboat, they learned of the British Band's movements. Within a matter of days, their mission had changed.

On April 12, Atkinson and his men landed at Rock Island and prepared to deal with the British Band. Although the true intention of the returning Indians was not clear to U.S. authorities at the time, most assumed that Black Hawk was behind it and that the Indians wanted war. Atkinson sent a messenger to the group, ordering them to go back to western territories. The general's arrival at Rock Island concerned the Sauks, but they dismissed his order. Black Hawk stated,

CORRESPONDENCE BETWEEN KEOKUK AND HENRY ATKINSON

On April 13, 1832, Brigadier General Henry Atkinson held a council with Keokuk and other headmen of the Sauks and Mesquakies. A week had passed since Black Hawk's band had crossed the Mississippi River. Atkinson wanted first to make sure that the Sauks and Mesquakies were not going to begin a war against the Sioux and Menominees. He also wanted to ensure that Keokuk and the others would not join Black Hawk. The following is an excerpt from Keokuk's speech in that council.

When Governor Clark went up, he invited those Indians over here [Black Hawk's band] to go up and they would not, my Chief would not go, I went up, I got a copy of the treaty, & explained it to my band, and also to the Rock river Indians, my village and the British band do not like each other, they will not listen to us, and that is the reason we do not know what to do. You say they must give themselves up, or the

"We were determined never to be driven, and equally so, *not to make the first attack,* our object being to act only on the defensive. This we conceived our right."[23]

During the next month, three different developments set the stage for the conflict that followed. Black Hawk realized that the British were not going to send supplies or any other support. As he and his people set up camp just north of Wabokieshiek's settlement, Black Hawk held a council. "I sent for my chiefs, and told them that we had been *deceived!* That all the fair promises that had been held out to us, through Ne-a-pope, were *false!*"[24] Although Black Hawk recognized this deception, he chose not to tell his followers.

Chief must do it, we can't give them up, it is out of our power, all of the Sacs engaged in the murder of the Menominees are off, or with the Black Hawk's Party; we are unfriendly to that Band, we will tell them what you say, last fall we had a meeting on invitation of Major Bliss and our Agent; as soon as the Council was over, those who are with Black Hawk's party went away, and we never could get them to speak with us since. If the War Party had started from our village, we would feel ourselves bound to give them up, but as it is, we are unable. You wish us to keep at peace, and have nothing to do with the Rock river Indians, we will do so in token of our intentions, you see we have lain our spears there altogether, while you are gone to the Prairie we will endeavour to speak to them, and try to persuade them to go back, if we do not succeed we can do no more, then we will go home, and try to keep our village at peace; the one who has raised all this trouble is a Winnebago called the Prophet.*

---

* Ellen M. Whitney, comp. and ed., *The Black Hawk War 1831–1832*, 3 vols. (Springfield: Illinois State Historical Library, 1973), 2:252.

Additionally, Atkinson refrained from using force, both because he did not believe the Indians were an immediate threat and because he did not think he had enough soldiers to confront the Indians. Atkinson was a frontier army veteran, and though he was adamant about making Black Hawk and his band leave Illinois, he was less inclined to accept the opinion that the Indians were preparing for all-out warfare.

The third development may have been the most important. In mid-April, Governor John Reynolds of Illinois called upon the state's citizens to form a militia. Stating that "the settlers on the frontier [were] in imminent danger," Reynolds ordered the militia to gather at Beardstown to repel the invading force.[25] The men of Illinois responded with enthusiasm, and by the end of April, the militia included more than 1,500 volunteers. Most, if not all, were eager to hunt down the Indians. In early May, they began their pursuit of Black Hawk.

The British Band was now encamped on the Kishwaukee River, northwest of Wabokieshiek's village and close to the present-day border with Wisconsin. Morale had begun to decline as food supplies ran low, and neither the local Ho-Chunk nor the local Potawatomi villages were willing to provide any corn or other assistance. Then, even as they met in council with a Potawatomi delegation on May 14, the leaders of the British Band received word that several hundred mounted soldiers were approaching.

Black Hawk sent three warriors with a white flag of truce and five others to observe events from a distance. The first delegation encountered a division of the Illinois militia under the command of Major Isaiah Stillman. The militiamen brought the three men into their camp and then grew suspicious when they saw the five others in the distance. Nervous, and perhaps a bit excited about the possibility of fighting Indians, the militiamen overreacted. They went after the five Sauk observers and fired upon them, killing at least one.

The violence that followed became known as the Battle of Stillman's Run. Having heard the news of the attack, Black Hawk had his warriors prepare for an assault by the militia. The Illinois citizen-soldiers were not prepared to face the more experienced Sauk and Mesquakie warriors. The attack quickly turned into a retreat, and the retreat turned into a defeat. Eleven militiamen and an unknown number of Indians died as a result. Just as important, the battle meant that there would not be a peaceful resolution to the British Band's return to Illinois.

CONCLUSION

The onset of conflict on May 14, 1832, was as much about confusion and ambition as anything else. Various descriptions of events leading up to the Battle of Stillman's Run present contrasting accounts. Many militiamen did not recall seeing a white flag of truce and declared that the Sauk delegations were clearly hostile. In contrast, some historians have argued that the militiamen were looking for an excuse to kill Indians before more U.S. soldiers arrived.

Black Hawk provided his own perspective several years later. "I had resolved upon giving up the war," he explained, "and sent a flag of peace to the American war chief . . . instead of this honorable course which I have always practiced in war, I was forced into WAR."[26] The native men and women who crossed the Mississippi in April 1832 had not done so with violent intentions. They were adamant about keeping their land and growing corn as they had always done, and they did not want war. After May 14, however, they found themselves in the middle of one.

The Road to the Bad Axe River

A MESQUAKIE MAN NAMED MAKAUK TALKED TO THE interpreter Antoine LeClaire on August 20, 1832, about his experience in the recent violence in Wisconsin. The Mesquakie was one of more than 100 prisoners held at Rock Island in the weeks after the final battles of the Black Hawk War. He told his story as part of a government report. "Eighty men—more or less escaped across the Mississippi," he shared. "We were so troubled about the women and children that I cannot tell exactly—six or seven days after we crossed we were attacked by the Sioux—counting men and boys about thirty escaped from them—all the rest were killed complete."[27] The specific events he described occurred in early August on the banks of the Bad Axe River, where it emptied into the Mississippi. Those were tragic days for the British Band and they marked the end of the pursuit that began following the Battle of Stillman's Run.

From May 14 to August 2, the British Band did everything it could to elude the Illinois militiamen and U.S. soldiers sent to defeat them. It was not an easy task. Rapidly declining food supplies and a lack of assistance from local Indian tribes complicated the efforts of Black Hawk and other leaders to hold the band together. Meanwhile, more than 3,000 militiamen and nearly 4,000 regular soldiers were called into action during those two months to pursue and capture the Sauks and Mesquakies.

The shots fired at Stillman's Run had ended any hope of a peaceful resolution as far as state and federal officials were concerned. After that initial encounter, the Americans prepared for war. Black Hawk and his followers realized that they did not have the numbers or the resources to fight the forces arrayed against them. And when it appeared that they would not receive any substantial assistance from the Potawatomis and Ho-Chunks in the region, the Sauks and Mesquakies searched for a way back across the Mississippi. For the sake of the women, children, and elders, the Indians wanted to avoid pitched battles. As a result, the incidents encompassed by the label of the "Black Hawk War" do not necessarily fit the title. What has been termed a war was more of a pursuit, and the final confrontation on the Bad Axe River was more of a massacre than a battle.

THE PURSUIT OF BLACK HAWK

In the days after the Battle of Stillman's Run, Black Hawk and his people were both confident and cautious. The Illinois militia had proven themselves to be cowards in the field, and the Sauk and Mesquakie warriors had little regard for these opponents. Yet they could not ignore the reality of their situation. "What was to be done?" Black Hawk asked years later. "It was worse than folly to turn back and meet an enemy where the odds was so much against us—and thereby sacrifice ourselves, our wives and children, to the fury of an enemy who had *murdered* some of our brave and *unarmed* warriors, when they were on a mission to *sue for peace*!"[28]

In May and June 1832, the Sauk and Mesquakie, among other Indian tribes, began a series of raids in Illinois. During this time, several white settlers were killed and some were kidnapped (depicted here) by these marauding groups.

Although the British Band did not want to turn and fight, they did not necessarily avoid conflict altogether. First and foremost they were desperate for food, and even as they made their way along the Rock River into present-day Wisconsin, the Sauks and Mesquakies raided frontier farms and settlements for livestock and other provisions. During the month after the Battle of Stillman's Run, Black Hawk even led a party of nearly 200 warriors in an attack against a fort and its surrounding settlement on Apple Creek in the lead-mining region of northwestern Illinois. Although the ensuing battle proved costly with the death of two Sauk chiefs, the Indians were able to obtain some food and other necessities from the cabins of local settlers.

The actions of the Sauks and Mesquakies in May and June also sparked raids by other Indians and created fears of a widespread Indian uprising in the region. On May 21, a war party of nearly 40 Potawatomis attacked a farming settlement in Illinois. They killed 15 people and kidnapped a pair of young women. Around the same time, a small party of young Ho-Chunk men arrived in the Sauk encampment with the intention of joining the fight against the Americans. In one of the raids that followed, the Ho-Chunk men killed the Indian agent Felix St. Vrain and three of his companions.

From late May to late June, Black Hawk's band stayed in the Four Lakes area near present-day Madison, Wisconsin. It proved a safe and secure place to hide, but it was not an ideal setting. Although the swamps and marshes of the region made it easier to elude their pursuers, it did not make it easy to find proper nourishment. "We were forced to dig *roots* and *bark trees*," Black Hawk reported, "to obtain something to satisfy hunger and keep us alive! Several of our old people became so much reduced, as to actually *die with hunger!*"[29] The British Band obtained some corn by trading with Ho-Chunks in the area, but even that was not enough. The situation finally became so severe that Black Hawk decided it was time to alter his plans. Worried that the pursuing U.S. forces might find and surround the encampment, and concerned about the consequences of further starvation, the Sauk leader determined that it was time to head back across the Mississippi River and return to the western lands.

Black Hawk had good reason to be concerned, because although the Illinois militiamen were not anxious to fight after having their first taste of battle, by late June the federal military forces had become more organized. The day after the humiliation of Stillman's defeat, Governor Reynolds had issued another call for volunteers. He asked for at least 2,000 more men to hunt down the Sauks and Mesquakies and any Ho-Chunks and Potawatomis who may have joined them. One newspaper, the *Galenian*, made a more graphic request, appealing to the each citizen of Illinois to "glut his steel and dye his hunting shirt purple with those monsters' blood."[30] But the passionate rhetoric did not match the spirit of the militiamen, who became disheartened by the lack of provisions and the difficulty of the task. Governor Reynolds recognized the problems and disbanded most of the militia in late May.

Even as the fervent calls for volunteers rose and then fell, federal officers assumed control of the military strategy. They had distanced themselves from the militia because they had little regard for the latter's fighting ability, discipline, and determination. The officers also realized that they needed to

THE HO-CHUNKS AND BLACK HAWK

In June 1832, General Henry Dodge employed a number of Ho-Chunk scouts to assess the location and strength of Black Hawk's band. One of these men was a Ho-Chunk named White Crow. In the excerpt below, White Crow talks about the relations between the Ho-Chunks and Black Hawk's band.

Father, you and this man [Mr. Cubbage] know that when you, he and I and our sister were at the Prophet's village in the month of April, I endeavoured to dissuade the Saukees from going up Rock river. But I could not succeed. When I spoke of going down to Rock Island to see White Beaver [General Atkinson] the Saukees tried to deter me from it, by telling me that the whites would hang me. But I had entire confidence in the whites and could not be intimidated. I went. The White Beaver took me by the hand and told me to go home and if the Saukees should come into my [word omitted] I must drive them out. They have come and I have not been able to drive them out. They came and we moved off from them, they followed, we moved and moved, till they have driven us out.

When I shook hands with White Beaver as I now do with my friend [Col. Hamilton] he said that he was glad that my heart was good and take action to combat the Indian raids and the rising panic among the civilian populations of the region. Brigadier General Atkinson had gradually organized his men and distributed some of them under the command of General Hugh Brady and some under Colonel Henry Dodge. He had also enlisted the services of several Potawatomi, Ho-Chunk, Sioux, Menominee, and Stockbridge Indians to serve as scouts.

Even with the organization of this force, however, Atkinson and his men continued to have problems locating the

my intentions pure. Altho' much suspicion has been entertained of us by many white persons, I declare before the Great Spirit, that my heart is good and my intentions pure. I always follow good advice. White Beaver told us to go home to our cornfields and hunting ground and there remain quiet. We did so and in a few days the Saukees came to us with their hands stained with the blood of your people and with the scalps of the slain. They told us that they had two of your sisters in captivity. We sent you word, and at your request we ransomed them and brought them to you in safety. Father, if we had been your enemies should we have done that?

We now ask you to give us some provisions for our families, we have been driven from place to place, we can neither hunt nor fish, and we have no corn fields, our women and children are nearly exhausted. Give us a wagon load of provisions, we will guard it out, and send a hundred of our young men to guard it back. Father, our circumstances are extremely embarrassing, for the Saukees are almost as mad with us as they are with you. They have tried almost every means in their power to involve us in difficulties with you. I expect that next they will kill some of our people, and try to make us believe it was you.*

* Ellen M. Whitney, comp. and ed., *The Black Hawk War 1831–1832*, 3 vols. (Springfield: Illinois State Historical Library, 1973), 3:695.

British Band. Criticism of the U.S. Army's inability to locate the Indians came from both local citizens and President Andrew Jackson. That situation soon changed. On July 3, Atkinson received word that his scouts had found signs of the British Band's trail near Lake Koshkonong in present-day southern Wisconsin. However, initial expeditions into the region were unsuccessful. Atkinson's frustration increased. Then, on July 19, a party of U.S. Army messengers happened upon the trail of the Sauks and Mesquakies as they headed west. After weeks of frustration and empty leads, the pursuit of Black Hawk began in earnest.

THE BATTLE OF WISCONSIN HEIGHTS

The armed forces under Colonel Henry Dodge led the pursuit of the British Band in late July. He and his men had first defended the lead-mining region and then moved farther into present-day southern Wisconsin under the orders of Atkinson. Now they set aside their fatigue and chased the Indians who had proved so elusive. The Americans quickly recognized that they were on the right path and that the Sauks and Mesquakies had grown desperate. It did not take experienced scouts to follow the trail, since everyone could easily spot the pots, blankets, and other equipment the Indians had tossed aside in their race to the Mississippi.

Black Hawk led his people northwest from the Four Lakes region to the Wisconsin River. The initial plan was to travel down the river until they reached the Mississippi and the safety that rested on the other side. Neapope and 20 men stayed behind the main party and kept their eyes open for any sign of Americans. They did not have to wait long, for Dodge's men quickly drew near and readied themselves for an attack.

On the afternoon of July 21, Black Hawk, Neapope, and 70 men prepared to meet the approaching soldiers. "We were now compelled to fight," Black Hawk asserted, "or sacrifice

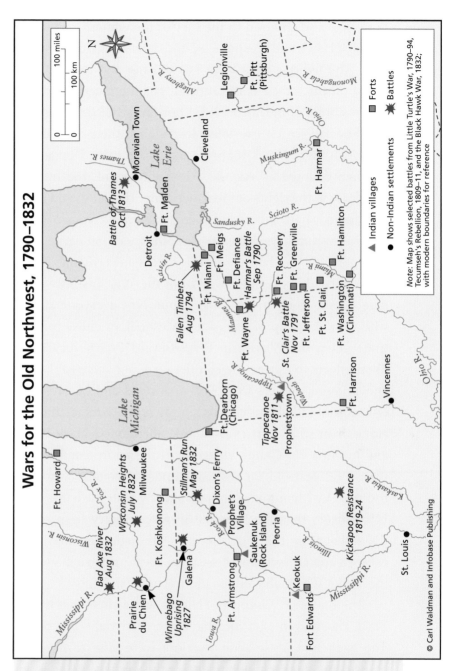

Wars for the Old Northwest, 1790–1832

The 1832 battles of Stillman's Run, Wisconsin Heights, and Bad Axe during Black Hawk's War marked the final Indian resistance in what once was the Northwest Territory. By 1833, many Indian tribes had been forced to move west of the Mississippi River.

our wives and children to the fury of the whites!"[31] Rain fell as Black Hawk and Neapope led the defense against Dodge's men. The fighting was fierce but did not last long. Dodge called off the attack as the sun set. His men were tired and the positions of both forces did not favor the U.S. soldiers. Yet they had struck a serious blow against the British Band. Although Black Hawk reported only six deaths, Dodge said his men counted at least 40. More important, the Indians were now in the sights of the Americans. The Sauks and Mesquakies may have succeeded in crossing the Wisconsin River, but they would have difficulty escaping their pursuers.

Following the battle and the successful crossing, Black Hawk turned his people away from the Wisconsin River to take a land route to the Mississippi. Not everyone stayed with him. A group of Sauks and Mesquakies chose to continue down the Wisconsin River toward Prairie du Chien. Their efforts to escape the conflict were not successful; they encountered soldiers from Fort Crawford and had to fight once again. Other individuals simply scattered and traveled alone or in small parties. Neapope abandoned Black Hawk and hid in a Ho-Chunk village until the entire conflict was over. A 50-year-old Sac woman named Weequaho, who was captured by Menominee Indians shortly after the battle, told U.S. officers that she "escaped in a temporary bark canoe down that river [the Wisconsin]."[32] Although some may have escaped and crossed the Mississippi River using such means, most, like Weequaho, ended up in American hands.

The Battle of Wisconsin Heights was a small victory for Black Hawk even as it foreshadowed the troubles to come. The Sauk and Mesquakie warriors were able to hold off Dodge's men long enough to enable the women and children to cross the Wisconsin. They lost lives in the process, however, and they still had many miles to go before they reached the Mississippi.

DEATH ON THE BAD AXE RIVER

On July 26, a military force of about 1,300 men crossed the Wisconsin River and began the final march in pursuit of the British Band. In the days after the battle at Wisconsin Heights, the situation had become even more desperate for the Sauks and Mesquakies, and the soldiers who followed in their path could see evidence of the Indians' troubles all along the route. "I witnessed scenes of distress and misery exceeding any I ever expected to see in our happy land," Colonel Robert Anderson wrote to his brother. "Dead bodies males & females strewed across the road . . . the elms . . . along the routes were barked to give them food."[33] The question was not *if* the soldiers would overtake the British Band, but *where.*

The flight of the Sauks and Mesquakies finally ended just south of where the Bad Axe River meets the Mississippi. The Indians reached the banks of the river on August 1, and by that time their numbers had dwindled to about 500 men, women, and children. Knowing that their pursuers were close behind, the remaining members of the British Band had to make a decision. Although Black Hawk wanted his people to head north to find shelter in the Ho-Chunk villages of Big Canoe and Winneshiek, most of the Sauks and Mesquakies wanted to cross the Mississippi as soon as possible.

While some individuals moved quickly to craft makeshift boats to cross the river, most never had the chance. On the afternoon of August 1, the steamboat *Warrior* traveled down the Mississippi and approached the Indians' position on the riverbank. The events of the 10 minutes that followed encompassed a number of misunderstandings. Black Hawk raised a white flag, hoping to board the boat to surrender. But language barriers and suspicion complicated any communication between the Indians on the shore and the men on the boat. Both the motives and the identity of the Indians were misunderstood, and the guns of the *Warrior* opened fire

The Battle of Bad Axe was a devastating blow to Black Hawk and the Sauks and Mesquakies. Already exhausted due to months of fighting, at least 300 of Black Hawk's people were killed and hundreds more taken prisoner in the conflict. Here, the U.S. steamer *Warrior* fires on a makeshift boat the Sauks had built to cross the Mississippi.

on the British Band. The Sauks and Mesquakies fought back as effectively as they could, and the skirmish ended when the *Warrior* headed to Prairie du Chien to refuel.

Following the departure of the steamboat, Black Hawk pushed once more for a movement to the north. Few listened to his advice. The elderly Sauk leader then made a critical decision and chose to take his family to the Ho-Chunk villages. Only three other families headed north with Black Hawk, and one of those included the family of Wabokieshiek. This meant that by the time night fell on August 1, 1832, Black Hawk, Wabokieshiek, and Neapope were no longer with the remaining encampment of the British Band. More important, the three leaders most responsible for the circumstances faced by their fellow Sauks and Mesquakies escaped the tragic events that unfolded on August 2.

After a long march on August 1, which brought them within a few miles of the Sauk and Mesquakie encampments, the U.S. soldiers rose before dawn on the next day to begin their attack. The soldiers were eager to fight, and almost every officer spoke later about the troubles they had in restraining their men. Although a party of Sauk and Mesquakie warriors attempted to lead the soldiers away from the main camp of the women and children, they were unsuccessful. As the Indians began their ill-fated attempt to cross the Mississippi River, the *Warrior* returned from Prairie du Chien and opened fire.

Both U.S. soldiers and Sauks and Mesquakies who survived later described the events of that day. There were many important differences in their descriptions, but the basic points could not be disputed. At least 300 men, women, and children died throughout the course of nearly 10 hours on August 2. Casualty rates among the U.S. forces were much lower. The Indians were tired, hungry, outnumbered, and outgunned. The U.S. forces were also tired, but they were simultaneously energized by the realization that their long chase had reached its conclusion. They were determined to make sure that the Indians did not escape.

In his report to his commanding officer, General Winfield Scott, Atkinson kept his description of the battle brief. Upon encountering the main body of Sauks and Mesquakies, "we attacked, defeated, and dispersed with a loss on his part of about one hundred & fifty men Killed 39 Women and children made prisoners." Atkinson was unable to provide precise numbers since "the greater portion were slain after being forced into the River."[34] Overall, he placed the casualties of the Sauks and Mesquakies near 300 and praised the efforts of his soldiers.

The onslaught was more devastating than Atkinson depicted in his brief note. As the soldiers descended the steep banks toward the Mississippi, some men and women pushed makeshift boats into the river in an attempt to cross. Other women hid in the tall grass along the riverbanks. Their attempts to hide often complicated matters. Anderson noted that "fighting with an enemy who concealed themselves in the high grass and behind logs and the banks of the ravines and river . . . required that our fire should be directed to every point where an Indian appeared."[35] In other words, there was little time or willingness to discriminate between armed men and unarmed women and children during the course of the battle.

Because of this devastation and loss of life, the voices of the survivors rarely described the conflict in the same way as the soldiers. Kekieequa, a 40-year-old Sauk woman, was one of the fortunate ones who hid in the grass and survived. She was captured after she "showed herself out of the grass to the Americans."[36] A somewhat more typical story of survival came from Namesa, a young Sauk women, who did not or could not give any details from the battle. She had "kept her infant close in her blanket by the force of her teeth—seized a horse's tail, and got across the Mississippi."[37]

Yet even those who managed to escape the U.S. forces did not reach safety. War parties from Wabasha's band of Dakota Sioux were waiting on the western side of the Mississippi River, and only a few days after fleeing the Americans, many of the Sauks and Mesquakies died at the hands of their traditional enemies. Once again the numbers are difficult to determine, but perhaps as many as 100 Sauks and Mesquakies escaped the chaos at the mouth of the Bad Axe only to lose their lives in the western lands they had tried so desperately to reach.

CONCLUSION

Upon hearing of the devastation on the Bad Axe River, Black Hawk mourned the loss of his people. He realized that he could do nothing more to aid his cause. After visits from several Indian delegations sent by U.S. officials, he decided to end further resistance. Accompanied by Wabokieshiek, Black Hawk surrendered to an Indian agent, Joseph Street, at Prairie du Chien on August 27, 1832. The Sauk leader's life was now in the hands of the federal authorities, and although he was imprisoned, his actions did not result in further punishment.

Those Sauk and Mesquakies who survived would not be so quick to forgive Black Hawk, Neapope, and Wabokieshiek. Nor could they forget who had led them down the path that ended on the banks of the Mississippi River. A Sauk-Mesquakie woman named Kishkashoi broke down and cried during her deposition with U.S. officials in late August 1832. When asked why, her response was clear: "All these names of chiefs who were the authors of all their troubles called up to her memory her six children whom she had lost by their bad advice."[38]

After the
Black Hawk War

IN EARLY SEPTEMBER 1832, BLACK HAWK TRAVELED BY steamboat down the Mississippi River as a captive of the U.S. government. He recalled one year later: "I surveyed the country that had cost us so much trouble, anxiety, and blood, and that now caused me to be a prisoner of war. I reflected upon the ingratitude of the whites, when I saw their fine houses, rich harvests, and every thing desirable around them; and recollected that all this land had been ours, for which me and my people had never received a dollar, and that the whites were not satisfied until they took our village and our grave-yards from us, and removed us across the Mississippi."[39]

During the next year, the federal government did everything it could to make sure that neither the Sauk leader nor his allies would trouble the United States again. In the process, Black Hawk also became a celebrity of the early nineteenth century. Although the final punishment was not as severe as what some citizens wanted—especially those in Illinois—President Andrew Jackson and his agents made sure that the Sauks and Mesquakies understood who held the power in the region.

Black Hawk's remarks bring out another important point about the relationship between Indians and Americans in the fall of 1832. His journey down the river opened his eyes to the flourishing settlements of whites along the waterway, and he could not help but think that the land hunger of the United States and its citizens would never be satisfied. This observation was not far from reality in the 1830s and the decades that followed. Yet Black Hawk was not fully aware of all of the consequences of the British Band's actions on the Indian populations throughout the Old Northwest.

Congress had passed the Indian Removal Act two years earlier, which meant that the relocation of eastern Indians had already been mandated. But the events of the Black Hawk War touched off a more determined push for removal among the U.S. citizens of the western Great Lakes region. And their efforts were not limited to the Sauks and Mesquakies. From the fall of 1832, into the 1840s, federal treaty commissioners, state officials, and residents of present-day Illinois, Wisconsin, Indiana, and Michigan arranged for land cessions and western relocations of Potawatomi, Ho-Chunk, and Miami bands. The conflict known as the Black Hawk War ended Sauk and Mesquakie hopes to retain their eastern territory. It also sparked a more widespread and passionate call for removal that affected Indian populations throughout the region.

BLACK HAWK'S TOUR

When Black Hawk and Wabokieshiek surrendered to Joseph Street at the Prairie du Chien Agency, there was a brief ceremony. Then Street turned the two men over to the custody of the military commander of Fort Crawford, Colonel Taylor. Several days later, the two leaders and a number of other Indian captives boarded a steamboat and headed south on the Mississippi River under the watchful eye of a young

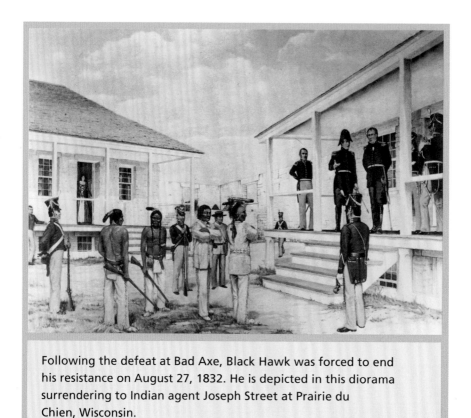

Following the defeat at Bad Axe, Black Hawk was forced to end his resistance on August 27, 1832. He is depicted in this diorama surrendering to Indian agent Joseph Street at Prairie du Chien, Wisconsin.

lieutenant named Jefferson Davis. As it turned out, the river journey to Jefferson Barracks in St. Louis would be the first of many travels for Black Hawk during the 11 months that followed. As a prisoner of the United States, he would see more of the country than he had ever seen in his previous 67 years.

The cells at Jefferson Barracks held only 11 men involved in the incidents of the recently ended conflict. The other captives had been released and allowed to return to the Sauk and Mesquakie villages in Iowa. Meanwhile, Black Hawk, his two sons, Neapope, Wabokieshiek, and six others spent the winter imprisoned and unhappy. They were placed in leg irons, a humiliation that Black Hawk found difficult to endure. "Was the White Beaver [General Atkinson] afraid that

I would break out of his barracks and run away?" he asked. "Or was he ordered to inflict this punishment upon me?"[40] When spring came, Black Hawk's wife and daughters, along with Keokuk, visited the prisoners. Keokuk petitioned for the release of Black Hawk and the other men, but the federal government denied that request.

Instead of freeing those individuals who were believed to have caused the war, President Andrew Jackson released only six and ordered that Black Hawk, his son Whirling Thunder, Wabokieshiek, Neapope, and Pamaho travel in custody to Washington. Thus began a three-month tour that made Black Hawk a celebrity throughout the eastern United States. Even during the first week, as the steamboat made its way up the Ohio River, crowds of curious onlookers assembled at the docks in Louisville and Cincinnati to get a glimpse of the Indian captives. Led by Lieutenant Thomas L. Alexander, the party stayed on the Ohio River until they reached Wheeling, West Virginia, where they disembarked and followed land routes by horse and by railroad the rest of the way to the nation's capital.

What Black Hawk and the other captives did not know was that the government intended to imprison them once more, this time at Fort Monroe in Virginia. President Jackson met the party in Washington but did not spend much time in conversation. Black Hawk remembered, "I had very little talk with him, as he appeared to be busy, and did not seem much disposed to talk."[41] Although the Sauk leader admired the president, he found it difficult to believe that the Indians would be incarcerated once more. All he and the others wanted was to return to their families, who were now living west of the Mississippi River. Instead they stayed at Fort Monroe, where they entertained numerous visitors, including artists eager to paint the infamous Black Hawk and Wabokieshiek.

Fortunately for the prisoners, Secretary of War Lewis Cass decided to end their confinement. He concluded that the situation among the Sauks and Mesquakies was by that time under control, and that Keokuk's leadership would not be disturbed by the return of those members of the British Band who had been perceived to be troublemakers. But there would be time for one final lesson. On their journey back to the Mississippi, the captives were taken through Philadelphia, New York, Boston, Albany, Buffalo, and Detroit. On this trip, Black Hawk and the others would have a chance to see firsthand the vast size and strength of the United States, and would understand the folly of going against the president's wishes in the future.

GEORGE CATLIN ON KEOKUK AND BLACK HAWK

From 1832 to 1839, George Catlin traveled throughout the United States visiting different Indian tribes. As he traveled, he painted and sketched a vast number of Indian men and women. His journeys included a stop among the Sauks and Mesquakies after the Black Hawk War. The following descriptions of Keokuk and Black Hawk are excerpts from the journal he kept of his journey.

Kee-o-kuk . . . is the present chief of the tribe, a dignified and proud man, with a good share of talent, and vanity enough to force into action all the wit and judgment he possesses, in order to command the attention and respect of the world. . . . His appointment as chief, was in consequence of the friendly position he had taken during the war, holding two-thirds of the warriors neutral, which was no doubt the cause of the sudden and successful termination of the war, and the means of saving much bloodshed. In his portrait I have represented him in the costume, precisely, in which he was dressed when he stood for it, with his shield on his arm, and his staff (insignia of office) in his left hand. There is no Indian chief on the frontier better known at this time, or more highly appreciated for his eloquence, as a public speaker, than Kee-o-kuk; as he has repeatedly visited

This second half of their expedition brought out much larger crowds than what had greeted the Indians in Louisville and Cincinnati. Black Hawk's fame even caused problems with another celebrity of the day. At a performance of the play *Jim Crow* at a Baltimore theater, the attention shown to the notorious Indian leader rivaled that given to President Jackson himself. "Black Hawk attracts almost as great a crowd as the President," one newspaper editor noted, "and resolving not to be outdone even by the General, he walks out upon

Washington and others of our Atlantic towns, and made his speeches before thousands, when he has been contending for his people's rights, in their stipulations with the United States Government, for the sale of their lands.

Muk-a-tah-mish-o-kah-kaik [Black Hawk] . . . is the man to whom I have above alluded, as the leader of the "Black Hawk war," who was defeated by General Atkinson, and held prisoner of war, and sent through Washington and other Eastern cities, with a number of others, to be gazed at.

This man, whose name has carried a sort of terror through the country where it has been sounded, has been distinguished as a speaker or councellor rather than as a warrior; and I believe it has been pretty generally admitted, that "Nah-pope" and the "Prophet" were, in fact, the instigators of the war; and either of them with much higher claims for the name of warrior than Black Hawk ever had.

When I painted this chief, he was dressed in a plain suit of buckskin, with strings of wampum in his ears and on his neck, and held in his hand, his medicine-bag, which was the skin of a black hawk, from which he had taken his name, and the tail of which made him a fan, which he was almost constantly using.*

* George Catlin, *Letters and Notes on the Manners, Customs, and Conditions of North American Indians*, 2 vols. (New York: Dover Publications, 1973), 2:210–211.

balconies, and bows to the multitudes with unceptionable [sic] grace."[42] Yet even Black Hawk grew tired of the continued attention. He was happy when the tour finally reached an end in early July 1833, and he was allowed to rejoin his family in a settlement on the Iowa River.

In the end, the tour served the purpose envisioned by Cass. The numbers of Americans who populated the eastern cities was at times overwhelming to the Indian captives. During the course of their journey, they were equally amazed by things such as railroads, hot air balloons, and the overall kindness of the white men and women who welcomed them at each place they visited. The end of the journey also brought sorrow, however, as Black Hawk viewed the increased settlements on the western side of the Mississippi River. "I am very much afraid," he stated, "that in a few years, they will begin to drive and abuse our people, as they have formerly done. I may not live to see it, but I feel certain that the day is not distant."[43]

THE SAUKS AND MESQUAKIES IN IOWA IN THE 1840s

Indeed, the drive of which the elderly Sauk had spoken began within a month of his surrender. While Black Hawk was still imprisoned at Jefferson Barracks and before he toured the eastern United States in his dual role as a prisoner of war and a celebrity, the headmen of the Sauk and Mesquakie villages west of the Mississippi sat down in council with General Winfield Scott and Governor John Reynolds. Scott and Reynolds had been appointed as treaty commissioners and they were charged with two assignments. First, they demanded payment from the Sauks and Mesquakies for the expenditures made by the United States during the recent conflict. Their second mission was to arrange for further land cessions from the Sauks and Mesquakies. Having concluded that the cause of the war was the closeness of the Indians to the white population, federal officials deemed it necessary for the Sauks and

Mesquakies to cede all of their territory along the Mississippi River. This would put more distance between the Indians and the citizens of Illinois and would theoretically decrease the possibility of further problems.

Keokuk, Wapello, and other Sauk and Mesquakie headmen sat in council with Scott and Reynolds from September 19 to September 21, 1832. During that time, they considered the government's offer of $600,000 paid out over 30 years for about 6 million acres located on the western side of the Mississippi River. Keokuk was the most vocal headman during the course of the negotiations. He knew that Scott and Reynolds were essentially dictating the terms of this accord. But he also recognized that the federal government wanted him to be the principal chief of the Sauk and Mesquakie. U.S. officials believed they could bypass Sauk and Mesquakie traditions and make Keokuk the sole leader of the remaining villages. Keokuk welcomed this idea, and took the opportunity to present a list of requests on the second day of the council. "The remainder of our lands is small," he noted toward the end of his speech. "The Sioux and others have been in the habit of hunting our lands. We wish you to guard us from their intrusions, and let us enjoy our land in peace."[44]

Keokuk spoke for all of the Sauks and Mesquakies when he asked that they be allowed to enjoy their land in peace. Yet his statement did not refer only to the dangers presented by the hunting parties of the Dakota Sioux. It also applied to the very real possibility that the U.S. government and its citizens would demand more territory in the future. Keokuk's concerns were justified, for the land hunger of settlers on the upper Mississippi River soon began to push the Indians farther west.

A second phase of Indian removal began in the western territories in the early 1840s, more than a decade after Congress passed the Indian Removal Act. At this time, the Sauk and Mesquakie population totaled about 2,300 people, who lived and hunted primarily along the Iowa and Des Moines rivers in the central part of the region. Iowa had become a U.S. territory in 1838, and with the passage of every year the number of non-Indian settlers increased. As these citizens clamored for more farmlands, the U.S. government approached the Sauks and Mesquakies to arrange for cessions of all of their territory.

In 1841, government commissioners visited the Sauks and Mesquakies and tried to arrange for a complete cession of their Iowa holdings. The Indians steadfastly refused to sell any part of their territory. Keokuk declared, "We were once powerful; we conquered many other nations, and our fathers conquered this land. We now own it by possession, and have the same right to it that the white men have to the lands they occupy." Other leaders made similar statements and expanded on Keokuk's comments. "We own this country by occupancy and inheritance,"[45] asserted Wapello, a Mesquakie headman. All those present rejected Commissioner John Chambers's proposal that they move farther west to the headwaters of the Des Moines River.

By the fall of 1842, however, the Sauks and Mesquakies could no longer ignore the persistent demands of the federal government. The pressure on the Sauks and Mesquakies to sell their land had increased exponentially due to the continuous stream of white settlers arriving in the territory. Both unable and unwilling to hold the settlers at bay, the U.S. government requested that Chambers once again attempt to negotiate. This time the Indians agreed to cede all of their lands in Iowa and to remove to present-day Kansas within three years.

The final negotiations lasted an entire week. On the second day of the proceedings, a Mesquakie named Kishkekosh addressed the Americans' thirst for lead, informing Chambers that the Indians had debated how much money they should demand for lands containing this resource. After Chambers rejected their initial offer to sell only a portion of their land, the Indians finally agreed to give away all of their

Kishkekosh, a Mesquakie leader, attempted to get the U.S. government to agree to pay them for their lands in Iowa, because they contained vast stores of lead. Unfortunately, by 1845, Kishkekosh and his people had been forced to leave Iowa and move to Kansas.

holdings in Iowa. Their experiences with treaty councils had made them better negotiators, and they tried to hold the commissioner to the offer made one year earlier of $1 million for their remaining acreage. They failed in this attempt, however, and three years later bands of Sauks and

Mesquakies began to move out of Iowa. It would not be the last time they moved.

INDIAN REMOVAL IN THE WESTERN GREAT LAKES

The Black Hawk War did not affect the Sauks and Mesquakies exclusively; nor was its impact limited to the Ho-Chunk, Menominee, and Potawatomi villages of present-day northwestern Illinois and southern Wisconsin. Both the fear of a widespread Indian uprising during the conflict and the push for removal after the violence on the Bad Axe River created ripples throughout the western Great Lakes region. From 1832 forward, the Anglo residents of the state of Indiana and Wisconsin (which became its own territory in 1836) made similar pushes to remove the Indian populations from those states.

In Indiana, federal and state officials focused their efforts on the Potawatomi and Miami settlements located north of and along the Wabash River. From 1832 to 1836, federal treaty commissioners signed nearly 20 different land cession treaties with Potawatomi bands living throughout the northern third of the state. The dispersed Potawatomi villages reflected the localized nature of political authority within the larger community. In other words, federal agents could not sign one treaty to arrange for the removal of all the Potawatomis from the region. During the course of the 1830s, therefore, small bands of Potawatomis relocated to present-day eastern Kansas in stages.

The removal of the Yellow River Band of Potawatomi was one of the most infamous of these forced relocations. It occurred at the same time as the Cherokee removal in the Southeast and is known as the Trail of Death. The Yellow River Potawatomis refused to recognize the validity of a treaty ceding their remaining lands in Indiana. As a result, they grew upset when white settlers began to cultivate the land near their villages. Isolated outbreaks of violence between settlers and Indians led Indiana's governor to call out the militia, and in September 1838, those militiamen rounded up nearly 800 Potawatomis. During the course of two months, the Indiana soldiers marched this band west. The Potawatomis buried nearly 40 men, women, and children on that journey.

The Miami Indians living on the Wabash River and its tributaries in northern Indiana experienced the same pressures faced by their Potawatomi neighbors. Treaty commissioners arrived hand in hand with the ever-increasing non-Indian population, and through the federal government's persistent efforts the Miami landholdings of almost 4 million acres in the early 1830s dropped to about 30,000 acres by the end of the decade. Then in 1840, Chief Jean B. Richardville signed an agreement stating that the Miamis would leave Indiana for new homes in the West within five years.

Because of repeated efforts by the Miamis to delay this relocation, the federal government finally took action. In early October 1846, U.S. soldiers used the threat of force to gather as many of the Miamis as they could, and forced them to board several canal boats in Peru, Indiana. After a journey of 27 days, during which about 16 Miamis died of sickness, 328 emigrants disembarked at present-day Kansas City via the steamboat *Clermont II*. On November 9, they arrived at their reservation after traveling 50 miles inland.

The interconnected stories of treaties and removals repeated themselves throughout the western Great Lakes region in the 1830s and 1840s. The Ho-Chunks ceded their entire lands southeast of the Wisconsin River in an 1832 treaty, and five years later agreed to remove to an assigned territory west of the Mississippi River. Although the relocation of the Ho-Chunks did not go exactly as planned by the treaty commissioners, by the late 1840s, the Ho-Chunk villages were largely relocated west of the Mississippi River.

Wisconsin entered the Union in 1848, and its white citizens did not include Indians in their visions for the future of the state.

CONCLUSION

The months and years after the end of the Black Hawk War revealed an interesting aspect of the relationship between the citizens of the United States and American Indians. Black Hawk, whose name had struck fear in the hearts of Illinois settlers in the summer of 1832, became a celebrity throughout the eastern cities in the spring and summer of 1833. He was all at once an oddity, an exotic individual, and a living Indian warrior at whom crowds of American citizens could gawk and admire from a safe and comfortable distance. In the latter stages of his journey, however, the crowds were not as friendly, and in Detroit a mob even burned Black Hawk in effigy.

American settlers in the western Great Lakes did not share the same romantic image of Black Hawk that had been crafted by their eastern counterparts. Instead they saw the elderly Sauk warrior as a prime example of the dangers posed by Indians on the frontier and the validity of western relocation. Therefore, the Black Hawk War was a catalyst and an example, a spark that furthered Indian removal in the region, and an illustration of why that removal was deemed necessary.

Icons and Indians in the United States

On a bluff overlooking the eastern bank of the Rock River at Lowden State Park in Oregon, Illinois, stands a sculpture that is nearly 50 feet tall and weighs at least 100 tons. The statue is that of an Indian man standing with his arms folded over his chest and looking out over the river. Its creator, Lorado Taft, sculpted the monument in 1911 and named it *The Eternal Indian*. Taft allegedly told his colleagues that the very stance of the statue made him think of Indians who had such a deep love for the environment and who must have often gazed upon the same landscape in days gone by. Despite the universal name Taft gave his creation, this statue has become associated with Black Hawk. And to residents of the region, the sculpture is said to suggest "a spirit unconquered while still a conquered race."[46]

Only 200 miles west of this statue is the Mesquakie Indian Settlement, located just west of Tama, Iowa. On this settlement of about 3,200 acres live more than 1,000 Mesquakie Indians. Their ancestors had returned to Iowa in the 1850s after losing their land in Kansas. They purchased an 80-acre

In 1911, artist Lorado Taft created *The Eternal Indian*, which many people believe represents Black Hawk. The statue, which stands nearly 50 feet tall, is located in Lowden State Park in Oregon, Illinois.

plot of land and gradually built up their community and acreage in the century and a half that followed. Although the strength of their traditional values has grounded their survival throughout the years, the Mesquakies have also taken advantage of opportunities to bolster the tribal economy. In late July 2006, they unveiled a new $110 million extension to their already successful hotel and casino operation. Iowa visitors and residents are able to play everything from bingo to poker, and the Mesquakie Nation and its members are benefiting financially from its operation.

The statue on the Rock River and the Mesquakie settlement in Tama provide a glimpse into a prominent issue faced by American Indians in the present day. It is a battle between the iconic Indian of the nineteenth century and the reality of the twenty-first century. *The Eternal Indian* is only one example of this larger struggle, as many non-Indians stubbornly hold on to the created images of men like Black Hawk and allow little room for the Indian men and women of today. The federally recognized tribes and nations of Sauks and Mesquakies have lived and continue to live with the consequences of the war of 1832 and the treaties that followed. Most reside far from the lands Black Hawk and others tried to retain, and they work hard to provide for the future of their people. It has not been easy, and the battle has been complicated throughout the past two centuries by those who refuse to give up a constructed or stereotypical image of American Indians, especially that of Black Hawk.

BLACK HAWK'S BODY

The creation and re-creation of Black Hawk as an icon started in the last years of his life and continued with the theft of his body shortly after his death. Black Hawk lived for five years after completing his journey through the cities of the eastern United States. Most of those five years were spent with his wife, two sons, and a daughter in a home along the Iowa River. Yet even as he tried to adjust to his new life west of the Mississippi, the elderly Sauk became a cult hero throughout the region. Visitors often arrived on his doorstep with gifts, and all of them hoped to meet and talk to the famous chief. It was safe to treat Black Hawk as a historical curiosity because there was no longer any reason to fear him.

A historian in the early twentieth century wrote that Black Hawk's postwar experiences created a misleading image of the Indian and the history of the conflict. "Those last few years," Frank Stevens asserted, "have been thus carelessly permitted to become the monument to the man, and those who drove him from power have been harshly judged."[47] Indeed, it did appear that residents of Illinois, Iowa, and Wisconsin were willing to overlook the past and viewed the former Sauk leader as either a hero or a martyr. Black Hawk was even the guest of honor at a Fourth of July celebration at Fort Madison, overlooking the Mississippi River. Those present toasted their famous guest, hoping that his days "be as calm and serene as his previous life has been boisterous and full of warlike incidents."[48]

Despite his continued celebrity status, Black Hawk had little if any authority among his people in the last years of his life, and he continued to blame Keokuk for his condition. He died on October 3, 1838, at the age of 71, and was buried aboveground in the traditional manner. His family placed him on a wooden board, one end of which was placed in the ground. Black Hawk wore a number of medals around his neck and he had three days worth of food and a pair of moccasins for his journey to the next world. Three other poles then provided supports for a mound built over the body with sod. The burial structure was designed in part to prevent animals from finding the body. But it could not prevent the assaults of humans.

In the summer of 1839, a man from Lexington, Iowa, named Dr. James Turner raided the grave and stole Black Hawk's remains. When notified by Black Hawk's family of the desecration, the governor of Iowa Territory led a passionate search for the culprit and the bones. Although the remains were recovered, they were not reburied. Instead they were given to the Geological and Historical Society Museum in Burlington, Iowa. The renowned Sauk leader would thus become an attraction in death as he had been in the latter years of his life. Then, when that building burned down in 1855, Black Hawk's remains were turned into ash along with the entire structure.

BLACK HAWK'S AUTOBIOGRAPHY

The construction of the iconic Black Hawk was not solely the work of outsiders. Before he died, Black Hawk displayed a personal interest in shaping the American public's perception of him and his people. From August to October 1833, Black Hawk dictated the events of his life to Antoine LeClaire, who was at the time employed by the U.S. government as an interpreter for the Sauks and Mesquakies. According to LeClaire, the elderly Sauk showed an interest in recording his life story after his return from the tour of the eastern United States. Black Hawk told his story to LeClaire, who translated it into English. A newspaper editor named John B. Patterson then prepared the resulting narrative for publication. It was the first Indian autobiography published in the United States and it continues to be an important resource for the historical period.

In the book's dedication, Black Hawk made clear his reasons for telling his side of the story. He addressed it to Brigadier General Henry Atkinson, the man who was responsible for the final defeat of the British Band more than a year before. "Before I set out on my journey to the land of my fathers," Black Hawk declared, "I have determined to give my motives and reasons for my former hostilities to the whites, and to vindicate my character from misrepresentation."[49] Having just returned from the tour of the eastern cities, Black Hawk knew that Americans were very interested in hearing his story. It is also apparent that he believed that his actions had never been understood clearly by the citizens of the United States. Specifically, he wanted Americans to know that he had always wanted peace and had been forced into war. His autobiography would therefore correct and counteract the false stories he may have heard during his time as a captive celebrity.

There has been a host of debates throughout the years about the authenticity of Black Hawk's autobiography. In 1835, an article in *The North American Review* stated about the work, "It is almost the only one we have ever read, in which we feel perfect confidence, that the author sincerely believes that every thing he has set down is the truth, the whole truth, and nothing but the truth."[50] Two decades later, an Illinois historian argued that Black Hawk knew little about the book and that it was merely a work of fiction created by LeClaire and Patterson. It is true that the work as published in 1833 is a story filtered through two different interpreters. Although it is impossible to know what may have been lost or added in the transfer of material from Black Hawk to Patterson, the accuracy and the insights provided in the autobiography appear to support its authenticity.

Neither those who have praised the book nor those who criticized it can escape the most important premise. The autobiography is not an unbiased account of Sauk history and the events of 1832. At its foundation it is a direct attempt by Black Hawk to present his version of events. He believed that he was misunderstood, and he knew that in 1833 he had lost his prominent position among his people. As much as it was possible, Black Hawk wanted to have a say in how he was viewed by people in 1833 and in the years that followed.

BLACK HAWK'S NAME

Although Black Hawk made an important statement with his autobiography, the appropriations of his name and image in the years since his death have usually overwhelmed his lone voice. For those who did not grow up in Illinois, Wisconsin,

Like many prominent Indians of the past, Black Hawk's name and image have been used in a variety of ways in American culture. Pictured here are members of the 86th Infantry Division of the Third Army, who are known as the Black Hawk Infantry Division, returning from action in World War II in June 1945.

or Iowa, the name Black Hawk does not always have a direct historical connection. During the course of the twentieth century, it has been affiliated with a number of different athletic teams, products, and geographic locations.

As is the case with many prominent Indians of the past, Black Hawk's name and image have been used in a variety of ways. At least four different U.S. naval vessels have been designated the USS *Black Hawk* and contemporary U.S. military operations often incorporate Black Hawk helicopters. Students can attend Black Hawk College in Illinois, drive through

Black Hawk County, Iowa, and stay at the Black Hawk Motel in Wisconsin Dells, Wisconsin. One of the more interesting references to the former Sauk in American pop culture comes in a song written by the musician Sufjan Stevens, entitled, "The Black Hawk War, Or, How To Demolish An Entire Civilization And Still Feel Good About Yourself In The Morning, Or, We Apologize For The Inconvenience But You're Going To Have To Leave Now, Or, I Have Fought The Big Knives And Will Continue To Fight Them." The song does not have any lyrics, but Sufjan's title delivers his message clearly.

Yet perhaps the most debated and well-known uses of Black Hawk are as a mascot. The use of Indians as mascots for college and professional athletic teams continues to be one of the most controversial and stereotypical uses of Indian images in the present day. Black Hawk has had a number of affiliations in this regard, though only one prominent connection remains. From 1946 to 1951, the Tri-Cities Black-hawks were the basketball team that represented the three cities of Davenport, Iowa, and Moline and Rock Island, Illinois. The team joined the National Basketball Association in 1949 and shortened its name to the Hawks in 1951, the name it still carries in Atlanta today.

The Chicago Blackhawks of the National Hockey League have not changed their name. In 1926, the new owner, Frederic McLaughlin, decided to rename the hockey team he had purchased. From his perspective, the team he had purchased, the Portland Rosebuds, did not have a proper name for a team about to join the National Hockey League. The inspiration for the team's new name came from a combination of McLaughlin's military experience and the team's new home in Chicago. According to the team history, "Members of his division called themselves Black Hawks in honor of the Sauk Indian chief who sided with the British in the War of 1812. Surely, the Major felt, it would be a fitting name for the newest entry into the National Hockey League."[51]

The idea of an Indian like Black Hawk as a fitting emblem for a professional hockey team is something that has resonated with hundreds of schools and professional athletic teams throughout the past century. Yet, even as many argue that such mascots honor the fighting spirit of the tribes or individuals of the past, others question how such images, especially those that are caricatures, show any respect to past or present American Indians. "Mascots don't live in the real world," author Carol Spindel points out, "but in the rarified imaginary space created by the overlapping bubbles of two of our most cherished American myths—sports and Indians."[52] Indeed, the use of Black Hawk's name for a sports team appears to display an unwillingness to recognize the problems of the past and the Indian men and women of the present.

BLACK HAWK'S PEOPLE

Instead of that "rarified imaginary space" to which Spindel refers, the Sauk and Mesquakie Indians reside in a world that the events of the nineteenth and twentieth centuries helped create. Both the size and the location of their homelands are an illustration of the impact of the summer of 1832 and the years that followed. Meanwhile, their contemporary political and economic status is a reflection of their persistence and strength in the face of federal impositions and policies.

As of 2007, three distinct communities of Sauks and Mesquakies have obtained federal recognition. All three are known officially by the federal government as the Sac and Fox, the designation imposed on these people since the treaties of the early 1800s. The Sac and Fox Nation of Oklahoma resides in the northeastern portion of that state, and the Sac and Fox Tribe of Missouri makes its home in northeastern Kansas. The third federally recognized group is the Sac and Fox Tribe of the Mississippi that resides on the Mesquakie settlement in Iowa. Of those three, only the land base of the Mesquakie settlement at Tama has grown during the past century. Each tribe or nation continues to make sure that outsiders understand that there are "three bands of Sac and Fox and they all have their own distinct government and enrollment processes."[53]

The Sac and Fox in Oklahoma are the descendants of the men and women who left Kansas after ceding their land through treaties signed in 1859 and 1867. Under the leadership of young Moses Keokuk, the son of the former principal chief, these Indians obtained their current territory in Oklahoma at the price of their lands in Kansas. They struggled to maintain the lands given in those treaties when Oklahoma became a state and as the federal government allotted Indian lands. As of the mid-1950s, only about 60 families still lived within the boundaries of the Sac and Fox Nation. In 2000, fewer than 100 men and women still lived in the vicinity, although more than 2,000 are on the enrollment lists.

The population numbers are even lower for the Sac and Fox of Missouri who reside in Kansas and Nebraska. Although enrollment in the tribe is more than 400, fewer than 60 live in the vicinity of the tribal lands. Like their relatives in Oklahoma, they live on the land that remains after a number of treaties in the mid-1800s and the allotment era of the late nineteenth and early twentieth centuries. More recently, they have taken advantage of Indian gaming regulations and run a casino in Powhattan, Kansas. They have also taken a proactive role in maintaining and telling their history through a tribal museum that opened in Reserve, Kansas.

The settlement in Iowa has the largest population of Mesquakies in the United States today. In the 1850s, the Mesquakies wanted to return to their former lands in Iowa, and they wanted to remove themselves from the influence of Keokuk, whose authority had grown with the assistance of the federal government. Although U.S. officials tried to force the Mesquakies to move south to Indian Territory, the Indians would not budge. They were supported by legislation passed

(continues on page 113)

The members of the Sac and Fox Nation of Oklahoma are descendants of those members of the tribe who ceded their land in Kansas after signing treaties in 1859 and 1867 with the U.S. government. Pictured here is tribal member Derrick Redbird, who is performing in the Grand Entry Dance at the Native American Pow Wow in Pasadena, California.

PRESERVING THE NATIVE LANGUAGE

Grace Thorpe, the daughter of legendary Olympic athlete Jim Thorpe, gave the following interview in 1994. In it, she discusses part of her childhood and points out a critical issue facing the Sauk and Fox today.

I never learned to speak our Native language. And Dad didn't speak it at home. Mother would not have understood. I don't know who he talked to. He'd have to sit there and talk to himself, except when he had visitors and relatives that would visit from time to time. When I was in my teens in Stockton, California, Dad was working for the motion picture industry as a casting director for Indians. During that period of time, I can recall many of our Sauk and Fox people coming to visit. And Dad and them would go back and forth all the time. Then when I'd come here to visit in Oklahoma with Dad, they would be speaking Sauk and Fox. But he just never spoke it with us at home, I'm sorry to say. I wish he had.

When the native language is no longer spoken, I feel that the thinking of the people in cultural terms is weakened. I suppose if you can speak your language, you are thinking in the language. It seems like it would change your whole thinking; the old way of life would soon be diminished. Fortunately, here with the Sauk and Fox, we do have language classes now. We did not have them when I came back here in 1976. So there has been a kind of renaissance and attempt to return to—to relearn—some of our old customs from some of the older people. There seems to be a resurgence of interest, among early middle age to middle age people who are really trying to get hold of our cultural heritage. Perhaps they see more of the importance of it as they become mature adults . . .*

---

* Rita Kohn and W. Lynwood Montell, eds., *Always a People: Oral Histories of Contemporary Woodland Indians* (Bloomington: Indiana University Press, 1997), 248–49.

(continued from page 110)

by the Iowa assembly in 1856 that gave them permission to remain in the state. By 1880, the population at Tama numbered about 355 people and encompassed almost 700 acres. At the beginning of the twenty-first century, the settlement included more than 5,000 acres.

CONCLUSION

Five months after the Mesquakies at Tama celebrated the addition to their new casino, they welcomed 20 new residents to their settlement. It took longer than expected, but in the first week of December 2006, the Mesquakies unloaded the bulls, cows, and calves that represented the first members of the Mesquakie tribal buffalo herd. A public ceremony would officially welcome these animals once they had adjusted to their new surroundings. Almost two centuries had passed and a great deal had changed since the Sauks and Mesquakies used the lands west of the Mississippi as hunting grounds during the course of their seasonal round. However, the descendants of the Sauks and Mesquakies of the nineteenth century are working to maintain and regain the traditions of their ancestors.

These connections to the past are also evident in the respect given to Black Hawk. In 1994, Grace Thorpe, the daughter of the famous Olympian Jim Thorpe, was the tribal district court judge for the Sac and Fox Nation of Oklahoma. Through her father she is a member of the Thunder clan, the same as that of Black Hawk. Her father was very pleased with that clan relationship. "Dad made the statement once that he was prouder of being in the same clan as Black Hawk than he was in winning at the Olympics in 1912," she remembered. "That gives you an idea of the stature that Chief Black Hawk has with me and many other members of the Sauk and Fox Tribe."[54]

Jim Thorpe, pictured here in 1931 with his daughter Grace, was a member of the Thunder clan; the same clan Black Hawk belonged to. The renowned Olympic athlete, who also played both professional baseball and football, was extremely proud to be related to Black Hawk.

Grace Thorpe and her father remembered Black Hawk as the man who led the last fight for the lands east of the Mississippi, and they were honored to have a clan connection to him. That is a very different honor from that proposed decades ago by the owner of the Chicago professional hockey team and maintained by athletic teams, hotels, and other entities in the present day. In the end, however, perhaps Black Hawk's autobiography provides the best route for remembering both his life and the lives of his descendants and their communities. When confronted in council and questioned about his position among the leaders of the tribe in June 1831, Black Hawk proclaimed, "I am a *Sac*! My forefather was a SAC! And all the nations call me a SAC!"[55]

Black Hawk was a man who acted in what he believed to be the best interests of his family, his nation, and his ancestors. He was not a perfect man. Nor was he a caricature. In all of these respects, he is not much different from the Sauks and Mesquakies of the twenty-first century who live with the legacy of those events of the summer of 1832.

Chronology

1767 Black Hawk is born at Saukenuk (near present-day Rock Island, Illinois).

1787 U.S. Congress passes the Northwest Ordinance.

1788 Mesquakies grant Julien Dubuque temporary rights to land on the western side of the Mississippi River.

1803 Louisiana Purchase made by the United States.

Timeline

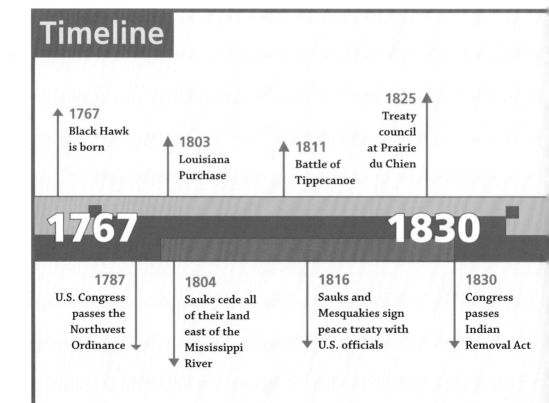

1767
Black Hawk is born

1803
Louisiana Purchase

1811
Battle of Tippecanoe

1825
Treaty council at Prairie du Chien

1767

1830

1787
U.S. Congress passes the Northwest Ordinance

1804
Sauks cede all of their land east of the Mississippi River

1816
Sauks and Mesquakies sign peace treaty with U.S. officials

1830
Congress passes Indian Removal Act

1804   Delegation of five Sauk Indians signs a treaty ceding all Sauk lands east of the Mississippi River.

1811   U.S. Army under William Henry Harrison defeats Indian confederacy under Tenskwatawa at the Battle of Tippecanoe (in present-day Indiana).

1812   War begins between British and U.S. forces; Black Hawk and others ally with the British.

1813   Several bands of Sauks and Mesquakies avoid the War of 1812 by moving west of the Mississippi River.

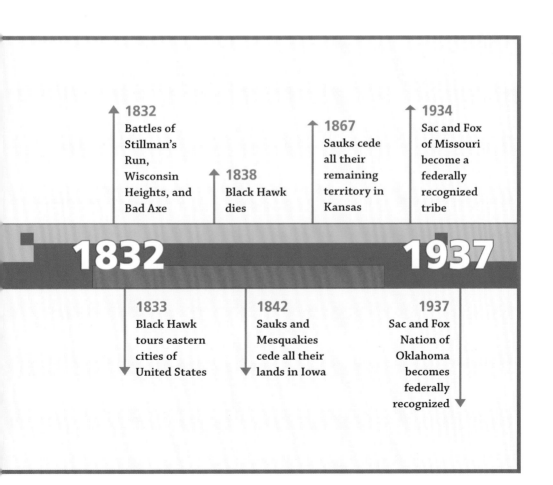

1832
Battles of
Stillman's
Run,
Wisconsin
Heights, and
Bad Axe

1838
Black Hawk
dies

1867
Sauks cede
all their
remaining
territory in
Kansas

1934
Sac and Fox
of Missouri
become a
federally
recognized
tribe

1832   **1937**

1833
Black Hawk
tours eastern
cities of
United States

1842
Sauks and
Mesquakies
cede all their
lands in Iowa

1937
Sac and Fox
Nation of
Oklahoma
becomes
federally
recognized

1816   Sauks and Mesquakies who allied with British negotiate and sign a peace treaty with U.S. officials.

1818   Illinois becomes a state.

1822   American miners set up camps along the Fever River (in present-day northwestern Illinois).

1825   Treaty council at Prairie du Chien takes place.

1827   Members of the Prairie La Crosse Band of Ho-Chunks attack settlers north of Prairie du Chien.

1829   U.S. government begins to sell Sauk lands on the Rock River.

1830   *MAY* Congress passes the Indian Removal Act.

1831   Six companies of infantry under Major General Edmund P. Gaines force Black Hawk's band to abandon Saukenuk.

1832   *APRIL 6* Black Hawk's band of Sauks and Mesquakies crosses the Mississippi River into Illinois.

        APRIL 15 Governor John Reynolds of Illinois calls out the state militia.

        MAY 14 British Band of Sauks and Mesquakies fight the Illinois militia during what becomes known as the Battle of Stillman's Run.

        JUNE 18 Battle of Kellogg's Grove, where 80 Sauk warriors fight a company of Illinois militia.

        JUNE 24 Black Hawk leads 200 Sauk men against a fort on the Apple River in northwestern Illinois.

        JULY 18 Scouts from Colonel Henry Dodge's force of volunteers and militia find a fresh trail from Black Hawk's band.

JULY 21 Dodge's men engage Black Hawk's band at the Battle of Wisconsin Heights.

AUGUST 1 Black Hawk's band reaches the Mississippi River at a point just south of the mouth of the Bad Axe River; the steamboat *Warrior* fires upon them; Black Hawk heads north to the Ho-Chunk villages.

AUGUST 2 Before dawn, U.S. soldiers under Atkinson attack the Sauks and Mesquakies still encamped on the banks of the river; fighting lasts for nearly eight hours and results in at least 300 Sauk and Mesquakie deaths.

AUGUST 27 Black Hawk and Wabokieshiek surrender to Joseph Street at Prairie du Chien.

SEPTEMBER Sauks and Mesquakies sign treaty that cedes land on western side of Mississippi River.

1833 *APRIL* Black Hawk, Neapope, Wabokieshiek, and three others begin their journey east to Washington, D.C.

JUNE 5 Black Hawk and other captives begin their tour of the eastern cities.

1838 *OCTOBER 3* Black Hawk dies.

1842 Sauks and Mesquakies sign a treaty that cedes their land in Iowa; they agree to remove to Kansas in three years.

1857 Mesquakie band purchases 80-acre plot of land near Tama, Iowa.

1859 Sauks in Kansas sign treaty ceding a portion of their reservation to the United States.

1867 Sauks in Kansas sign a treaty ceding their remaining lands in that state.

1896 State of Iowa surrenders its jurisdictional authority over the settlement of Mesquakie Indians at Tama to the federal government.

1934 Sac and Fox of Missouri become a federally recognized tribe under the Indian Reorganization Act.

1937 Sac and Fox Nation of Oklahoma ratifies a constitution that marks them as a federally recognized tribe.

1996 Sac and Fox Nation of Missouri opens tribal museum and research center in Reserve, Kansas.

2006 Sac and Fox tribe of the Mississippi in Iowa unveil a new $110 million extension to their successful hotel and casino in Tama, Iowa.

Notes

Chapter 1

1. Francis Paul Prucha, ed., *Documents of United States Indian Policy* (Lincoln: University of Nebraska Press, 1990), 15–16.
2. Albert L. Hurtado and Peter Iverson, eds., *Major Problems in American Indian History* (Lexington, Mass.: D.C. Heath and Company, 1994), 169.

Chapter 2

3. Donald Jackson, ed., *Black Hawk: An Autobiography* (Urbana-Champaign, Ill.: University of Illinois Press, 1987), 41.
4. Prucha, *Documents of United States Indian Policy*, 22.
5. Charles Kappler, comp. and ed., *Indian Affairs: Laws and Treaties*, vol. 2, *Treaties* (Washington, D.C.: U.S. Government Printing Office 1904), 74.
6. Kerry A. Trask, *Black Hawk: The Battle for the Heart of America* (New York: Henry Holt and Company, 2006), 73.
7. Jackson, *Black Hawk*, 64.

Chapter 3

8. Thomas Forsyth, "An Account of the Manners and Customs of the Sauk and Fox Nations of Indians Tradition," in *The Indian Tribes of the Upper Mississippi Valley and Region of the Great Lakes*, ed. Emma Helen Blair, 2:236 (Lincoln: University of Nebraska Press, 1996).
9. Letter of Sacs and Foxes to William Clark, May 24, 1830, National Archives Record Group 75, Office of Indian Affairs, Letters Received, roll 747.
10. Lucy Eldersveld Murphy, *A Gathering of Rivers: Indians, Metis, and Mining in the Western Great Lakes, 1737–1832* (Lincoln: University of Nebraska Press, 2000), 84.
11. Ibid., 96.
12. Ibid., 129.

Chapter 4

13. Jackson, *Black Hawk*, 107.
14. Ibid., 49.
15. Ibid., 139.
16. Ellen M. Whitney, comp. and ed., *The Black Hawk War 1831–1832*, 3 vols. (Springfield, Ill.: Illinois State Historical Library, 1973), 2:157.
17. Jackson, *Black Hawk*, 101.

Chapter 5

18. Ibid., 107.
19. Ibid., 108.
20. Ibid., 111.
21. Ibid., 117.
22. Ibid., 118.
23. Ibid., 120.
24. Ibid., 121–122.
25. Trask, *Black Hawk*, 162.
26. Jackson, *Black Hawk*, 126–127.

Chapter 6

27. Whitney, *The Black Hawk War*, 2:1036.
28. Jackson, *Black Hawk*, 127.
29. Ibid., 133.
30. Trask, *Black Hawk*, 194.
31. Jackson, *Black Hawk*, 134.
32. Whitney, *The Black Hawk War*, 3:1030.
33. Ibid., 3:933.
34. Ibid., 3:935.
35. Ibid., 3:933.
36. Ibid., 3:1032.
37. Ibid., 3:1035.
38. Ibid., 3:1029–1030.

Chapter 7

39. Jackson, *Black Hawk*, 141–142.
40. Ibid., 142.
41. Ibid., 145.
42. Trask, *Black Hawk*, 300.
43. Jackson, *Black Hawk*, 150.
44. Whitney, *The Black Hawk War*, 3:1172.
45. Minutes of a treaty held at the Sac and Fox Indian agency in October 1841, Report of the Commissioner of Indian Affairs, 1841.

Chapter 8

46. "Oregon Sculpture Trail," City of Oregon, Illinois. Available online at *http://www.oregonil. com/scupture-trail.html* (accessed February 12, 2007).
47. Cyrenus Cole, *I Am a Man: The Indian Black Hawk* (Iowa City: The State Historical Society of Iowa, 1938), 267.
48. Ibid., 269.
49. Jackson, *Black Hawk*, 37.
50. Ibid., 25.
51. "The McLaughlin Years," The Chicago Black Hawks. Available online at *http://www. chicagoblackhawks.com/ history/TheMcLaughlinYears. asp* (accessed February 12, 2007).
52. Carol Spindel, *Dancing at Halftime: Sports and the Controversy over American Indian Mascots* (New York: New York University Press, 2000), 18.
53. "Tribal History," Sac & Fox Casino, Available online at *http://www.sacandfoxcasino. com/tribal-history.html* (accessed February 12, 2007).
54. "Grace Thorpe," in *Always a People: Oral Histories of Contemporary Woodland Indians*, eds. Rita Kohn and W. Lynwood Montell (Bloomington: Indiana University Press, 1997), 247.
55. Jackson, *Black Hawk*, 111.

Bibliography

Blair, Emma Helen. *The Indian Tribes of the Upper Mississippi Valley and Region of the Great Lakes*. Lincoln: University of Nebraska Press, 1996.

Cole, Cyrenus. *I Am a Man: The Indian Black Hawk*. Iowa City: The State Historical Society of Iowa, 1938.

Dowd, Gregory Evans. *A Spirited Resistance: The North American Indian Struggle for Unity, 1745–1815*. Baltimore: The Johns Hopkins University Press, 1992.

Foreman, Grant. *Indian Removal: The Emigration of the Five Civilized Tribes of Indians*. Norman: University of Oklahoma Press, 1932.

Hagan, William T. *The Sac and Fox Indians*. Norman: University of Oklahoma Press, 1958.

Horsman, Reginald. *Expansion and American Indian Policy, 1783–1812*. Norman: University of Oklahoma Press, 1992.

Hurtado, Albert L., and Peter Iverson, eds. *Major Problems in American Indian History*. Lexington, Mass.: D.C. Heath and Company, 1994.

Jackson, Donald, ed. *Black Hawk: An Autobiography*. Urbana-Champaign: University of Illinois Press, 1987.

Kappler, Charles, comp. and ed. *Indian Affairs: Laws and Treaties*. Vol. 2, *Treaties*. Washington, D.C.: U.S. Government Printing Office, 1904.

Kohn, Rita, and W. Lynwood Montell, eds. *Always a People: Oral Histories of Contemporary Woodland Indians*. Bloomington: Indiana University Press, 1997.

Lappas, Thomas J. "A Perfect Apollo." In *The Boundaries Between Us: Natives and Newcomers along the Frontiers of the Old Northwest Territory, 1750–1850*, edited by Daniel P. Barr. Kent, Ohio: Kent State University Press, 2006.

Lewis, James. "The Black Hawk War of 1832." Northern Illinois University, Abraham Lincoln Historical Digitization Project. Available online at *http://lincoln.lib.niu.edu/blackhawk/index.html*.

Murphy, Lucy Eldersveld. *A Gathering of Rivers: Indians, Metis, and Mining in the Western Great Lakes, 1737–1832*. Lincoln: University of Nebraska Press, 2000.

Nichols, Roger L. *Black Hawk and the Warrior's Path*. Arlington Heights, Ill.: Harlan Davidson, 1992.

Prucha, Francis Paul, ed. *Documents of United States Indian Policy*. Lincoln: University of Nebraska Press, 1990.

Spindel, Carol. *Dancing at Halftime: Sports and the Controversy over American Indian Mascots*. New York: New York University Press, 2000.

Tanner, Helen Hornbeck, ed. *Atlas of Great Lakes Indian History*. Norman: University of Oklahoma Press, 1987.

Trask, Kerry A. *Black Hawk: The Battle for the Heart of America*. New York: Henry Holt and Company, 2006.

Whitney, Ellen M., comp. and ed. *The Black Hawk War 1831–1832*. 3 vols. Springfield: Illinois State Historical Library, 1973.

Wisconsin Historical Society. "The Black Hawk War." Available online at *http://www.wisconsinhistory.org/turningpoints/tp-012*.

Further Reading

Deloria, Philip J. *Playing Indian*. New Haven: Yale University Press, 1998.

Edmunds, R. David, and Joseph L. Peyser. *The Fox Wars: The Mesquakie Challenge to New France*. Norman: University of Oklahoma Press, 1993.

Hurt, R. Douglas. *The Indian Frontier, 1763–1846*. Albuquerque: University of New Mexico Press, 2002.

Wallace, Anthony F. C. *The Long, Bitter Trail: Andrew Jackson and the Indians*. New York: Hill & Wang, 1993.

WEB SITES

The Black Hawk War of 1832
http://lincoln.lib.niu.edu/blackhawk/index.html

Sac and Fox Tribe of the Mississippi in Iowa
http://www.meskwaki.org/

Sac and Fox Nation of Oklahoma
http://www.sacandfoxnation-nsn.gov/index.htm

The Black Hawk War
http://www.wisconsinhistory.org/turningpoints/tp-012/

Picture Credits

Index

About the Contributors

Author **JOHN P. BOWES** is assistant professor of Native American History at Eastern Kentucky University. His other projects include *Exiles and Pioneers: Eastern Indians in the Trans-Mississippi West*, forthcoming from Cambridge University Press in 2007 as part of its series Studies in North American Indian History. *Exiles and Pioneers* examines the removal and postremoval experience of the Shawnee, Delaware, Wyandot, and Potawatomi Indians from the late 1700s to the 1870s. Bowes received a B.A. in history from Yale University and completed both his M.A. and Ph.D. in history at the University of California at Los Angeles.

Series editor **PAUL C. ROSIER** received his Ph.D. in American history from the University of Rochester in 1998. He currently serves as assistant professor of history at Villanova University, where he teaches Native American history, the environmental history of America, history of American Capitalism, and world history. Dr. Rosier is the author of *Rebirth of the Blackfeet Nation, 1912–1954* (2001) and *Native American Issues* (2003). His next book, on post–World War II Native American politics, will be published in 2008 by Harvard University Press. Dr. Rosier's work has appeared in various journals, including the *Journal of American History*, the *American Indian Culture and Research Journal*, and the *Journal of American Ethnic History*.